Contents

Introduction 1

Unit 1 Election campaigns and voting behaviour
   A Models of voting behaviour 5
   B Other influences on voting behaviour 7
   C The general election of 2001 9

Unit 2 Elections, electoral reform and referendums
   A The electoral system in the UK 13
   B The first-past-the-post system 16
   C Other electoral systems 18
   D Referendums 21
   E Key terms and concepts 22

Unit 3 The prime minister
   A Evolution of the office of prime minister 24
   B Sources of the prime minister's power 26
   C The powers of the prime minister 27
   D Limits on a prime minister's power 31
   E Prime ministerial styles 32
   F Debates on prime ministerial power 33
   G Key terms and concepts 35

Unit 4 The cabinet
   A Development of the cabinet 36
   B Aspects of the modern cabinet 36

Unit 5 Ministers
   A Different types of government minister 40
   B The role of ministers 41
   C Ministerial responsibility 42
   D Ministerial turnover 43

Unit 6 The civil service, agencies and quangos
   A Development of the civil service 45
   B Aspects of the modern civil service 50
   C The non-civil service 51

Unit 7 Parliament: the House of Commons
A The development of parliament 53
B Functions of the House of Commons 54
C Members of Parliament 54
D The role of party 56
E The role of the opposition 57
F How laws are made 57
G The role of standing and select committees 59
H The scrutiny role of the House of Commons 61
I Some important issues 62
J Key terms and concepts 63

Unit 8 Parliament: the House of Lords
A Development of the House of Lords 64
B The present composition of the House of Lords 65
C The present role of the House of Lords 65
D Criticisms of the House of Lords 66
E Reform of the House of Lords 67
F Key terms and concepts 69

Unit 9 Political parties
A The Conservative Party 70
B The Labour Party 72
C Leadership selection 76
D Selection of parliamentary candidates 76
E The role of party conferences 78
F The role of party leaders 79
G Funding of political parties 80
H Declining party membership 82
I The role of political parties 82
J Key terms and concepts 83

Unit 10 Pressure groups
A What is a pressure group? 85
B Types of pressure group 85
C The role of pressure groups 88
D Pressure group methods 90
E Reasons for pressure group success 91
F The growth and spread of pressure politics 91
G Key terms and concepts 92

the

AS
UK Government and Politics

Patrick Walsh-Atkins

Exam
Revision
Notes

Philip Allan Updates
Market Place
Deddington
Oxfordshire
OX15 0SE

tel: 01869 338652
fax: 01869 337590
e-mail: sales@philipallan.co.uk
www.philipallan.co.uk

ISBN 0 86003 436 4

Cover illustration by John Spencer
Printed by Raithby, Lawrence & Co. Ltd, Leicester

Unit 11 The European Union and the United Kingdom

A The European Union and British involvement 93
B Key European treaties.. 95
C Key institutions of the European Union... 98
D The impact of the European Union on the United Kingdom............................. 100
E Attitudes of the major political parties 101
F Key terms and concepts.. 102

Unit 12 The judicial system

A The role of the judiciary in the United Kingdom.. 105
B Judges and the political process.. 107
C Key terms and concepts.. 108

Unit 13 The British constitution

A Origins and development of the British constitution.. 110
B The main sources of the British constitution... 112
C Principles of the British constitution 115
D The constitution: a major issue 116
E Key terms and concepts.. 118

Unit 14 Citizenship, rights and the redress of grievances

A Citizenship.. 120
B Rights and liberties... 121
C Defence of rights and liberties in the UK 123
D Key terms and concepts.. 126

Introduction

About this book

Before you use this revision book you should have already:

- made use of the recommended textbook(s)
- made your own detailed notes on all the key topics that form the core of the AS specification
- found up-to-date examples of political events (e.g. a backbench revolt against a government) that can illustrate points you may make in your answers
- looked carefully at the past papers for the *new* AS examinations
- practised past papers under timed conditions, so you are aware of how much time can be allocated to each question and sub-question
- checked that you know exactly how marks are allocated in the exam papers
- checked a copy of the specification of the examination board you are following to ensure that you have covered all the compulsory material
- read carefully the relevant 'Teacher Guide' for AS government and politics, which all three major examination boards publish. They can be a little 'wordy', but they contain a lot of vital material. If your school or college does not have a copy, you can get one direct from the examination board.

This book is designed for use as a revision guide to clarify the course and to prepare you for the AS examination. It will also be very useful when you are preparing for the 'synoptic' paper at A2 in the second year of the course. When you have covered a topic (e.g. pressure groups), just check the revision material here to ensure that all aspects of the topic have been covered.

All the topics listed in the content specification of the three major examination boards are covered here. The layout is designed to enable you to prepare for the types of question you will get in the exam.

About the AS examination

At the time of writing (August 2001) all three major boards require candidates to take three separate papers lasting between 1 and 1½ hours each. Usually two papers will be taken on the same day. This may change for June 2002.

Marks are allocated in a very straightforward manner, and candidates are well advised to learn carefully exactly how many marks are allocated and how they are allocated in each question and in each paper. The specification published by each examination board lists the allocation of marks precisely, and this allocation should be noted very carefully.

AS government and politics has three 'Assessment Objectives', and marks are allocated to each one of these objectives. The Assessment Objectives are as follows:

Assessment Objective 1 (AO1)	Factual knowledge
Assessment Objective 2 (AO2)	Analysis/evaluation/argument
Assessment Objective 3 (AO3)	Quality of communication/grammar/spelling, etc.

So a question offering a total of 50 marks might have its marks allocated like this:

AO1   20 marks
AO2   20 marks
AO3   10 marks

You can see why it is vital to find out how the marks are allocated for each question.

If the marks are allocated as in the example above, you need to ensure that you have not just listed factual knowledge (and gained the AO1 marks). In order to gain the AO2 marks, there should be clear evidence that you have argued, analysed and evaluated. Similarly, however brilliant you are at arguing a case, you cannot get more than 20 marks for it; you must include some facts to back up your argument.

You must also remember that a significant number of marks are allocated to AO3. This covers not just spelling, grammar and punctuation, but also quality of explanation and communication. A candidate who writes good English and can also clearly explain complex ideas, such as sovereignty, will get high marks here. For two of the examination boards, *20%* of the marks are allocated to AO3, so care with communication can make *at least one grade's difference.*

Candidates can expect three different types of question in AS government and politics.
- **Stimulus material.** In some papers you may be given stimulus material, which will set the scene for a topic and possibly assist with ideas.
- **Data-response.** In other papers you will be given data, such as statistics from recent elections, and asked questions based on those data. You will be expected to apply some 'own knowledge' as well.
- **Mini essays.** Other exam papers will require 'mini essays'. None of the examination boards expects full essays of the traditional type at AS.

Example of a data-response question

Using the data in Source B, and your own knowledge, what conclusions can be drawn about the UK electoral system?   *(30 marks)*

The mark allocation here might be AO1 (factual knowledge), 24 marks and AO3 (communication), 6 marks. Of the 24 AO1 marks, about 12 will be allocated to using the data intelligently, and about 12 to using your own knowledge. The sensible way to manage such a question would be to answer it in two separate paragraphs, one clearly using the data given in the exam paper, and the other very obviously using *additional* knowledge. This will make it much easier to mark!

Examples of mini-essay questions

1 What is meant by collective ministerial responsibility?   *(10 marks)*

Only a small amount of time should be allocated to this question — enough to produce a short paragraph at the most. Only AO1 and AO3 marks are allocated for this type of question, so don't get involved in a long argument about the merits and demerits of collective ministerial responsibility. Just explain clearly what you understand by it (don't confuse it with *individual* ministerial responsibility) and remember that the AO3 marks will be awarded partly for the quality and clarity of your explanation, and partly for the quality of the English used. It is always a good idea to add one or two recent examples (at most) to demonstrate your understanding of collective ministerial responsibility.

2 Outline an argument against the use of referendums.   *(30 marks)*

The mark allocation here might be: AO1, 8 marks; AO2, 16 marks; AO3, 6 marks. Don't consider making a case 'for'. The way to get the marks is to focus on the argument against referendums. Make five or six points 'against' (they are listed in the book). Don't be concerned about making it a strong argument — there is no 'right or wrong' in political argument.

Back up your points with detailed examples, possibly drawn from the recent referendums on devolution and London, which will obtain the AO1 marks. If you feel that there is one overwhelming point 'against', then say so, and explain why you feel it is the 'key' point — you will get AO2 marks for that. Don't worry about writing an introduction or a conclusion. You don't have time for them — no examination expects elaborate essays to be written in 25 minutes.

3 Explain the case for reforming the way in which political parties are funded.

(30 marks)

This was actually set in the January 2001 examination for one board. The mark allocation was: AO1, 12 marks; AO2, 12 marks; AO3, 6 marks. The candidates who got full marks made three or four clear points (the AO2 marks) as to why the present system was felt to be unsatisfactory (and did not waste time trying to defend it!). They backed up their points with good recent knowledge (the AO1 marks) about how parties gained their funds and how much, and also made reference to major recent political events such as the Ecclestone affair. With a clearly explained case written in good English, it was not difficult to get all 30 marks.

Election campaigns and voting behaviour

This is a central topic for two of the examination boards, AQA and OCR. Both have modules in which candidates are certain to get a compulsory question on elections and voting behaviour, and it is essential that candidates for those two boards have a thorough and detailed knowledge of this topic. In particular, a good working knowledge of the 2001 and 1997 elections is called for. Edexcel candidates require only outline knowledge of this topic, as it is not stressed in Edexcel's content specification.

Key questions

What are the factors behind voting behaviour?

Assess the effect of election campaigns and opinion polls on the outcomes of general elections.

What role do the media play in winning or losing elections?

How important is social class in voting behaviour?

A Models of voting behaviour

Knowledge of the main theories, or models, offered by experts to explain individual citizens' votes is required. The main theories are described below.

PARTY IDENTIFICATION

This suggests that voters identify with a party at a young age and remain loyal to it in voting terms throughout their lives. The voter might in exceptional circumstances vote for another party. The reason for the early identification with one party tends to be social and economic. However, this is seen as very much a declining factor in voting behaviour. It influenced over 90% of voters in 1951 and only about 55% in 1997. This drop in class identification with a party is known as **party dealignment**. Better education, less thinking in class terms and a poor perception of parties are seen as the causes of this drop in automatic party support.

SOCIAL CLASS

Experts in the 1960s and 1970s saw this as a major factor. The majority of classes A, B and C1 voted Conservative, while the majority of classes C2, D and E voted Labour. However, what is known as **class dealignment** (where voters do not see themselves as members of a particular social class or identify with it) has been taking place. Statistics for the 1992 and 1997 elections (see Table 1.1) show this.

Note that when the Conservatives won in 1992 a significant number of the 'higher' social classes voted Labour and a significant number of the 'lower' social classes voted Conservative. This shows that although class is an issue, it is certainly not a dominant one. Fewer and fewer voters think of themselves as part of a 'class'.

	AB		C1		C2		DE	
	1992	1997	1992	1997	1992	1997	1992	1997
Conservative	53	42	48	26	40	25	29	21
Labour	22	31	28	47	39	54	52	61

Table 1.1 Social class and voting behaviour, 1992 and 1997 (%)

GENDER, AGE AND ETHNICITY

Table 1.2 gives figures for voting behaviour in 1992 and 1997 according to gender, age and ethnicity.

Gender	Conservative		Labour	
	1992	1997	1992	1997
Men	38	31	36	44
Women	44	32	34	44

Age	Conservative		Labour	
	1992	1997	1992	1997
18–24	38	22	35	56
25–34	37	25	41	50
35–44	38	26	38	53
45–64	44	29	35	44
65+	49	36	33	44

Ethnicity	Conservative		Labour	
	1992	1997	1992	1997
Black and Asian voters	10	17	78	81

Table 1.2 Gender, age, ethnicity and voting behaviour (%)

Black and Asian voters make up about 5% of the population, but their vote tends to be concentrated in specific areas.

REGIONAL FACTORS

The key statistics on regional voting behaviour are given in Table 1.3. This time the fortunes of the Liberal Democratic and the nationalist parties are included.

RATIONAL CHOICE

This model of voting behaviour argues that voters make up their minds not because of the class they belong to, or their age, but by exercising a rational choice based on the records of the parties, the policies offered in their manifestos and voters' perceptions of the party leaders and the possible members of their cabinets.

RECENT THEORIES BASED ON ELECTIONS 1979-97

- **Issue voting.** This argues that voters vote either because they like the policies of one party (e.g. the privatisation and tax cutting of the Conservatives in the 1980s, or the increased spending on health and education of Labour), or because they dislike the policies of a particular party.

Region	Conservative		Labour		Liberal Democrat		Nationalist	
	1992	1997	1992	1997	1992	1997	1992	1997
North	33	22	51	61	11	13	–	–
North West	36	26	45	54	16	15	–	–
West Midlands	45	34	39	48	15	14	–	–
South West	48	37	19	26	31	31	–	–
South East	54	41	21	32	23	21	–	–
Yorkshire and Humberside	38	28	52	58	16	15	–	–
East Midlands	46	35	48	58	15	13	–	–
East Anglia	51	39	38	48	20	18	–	–
London	45	31	36	49	15	14	–	–
Wales	29	20	43	55	12	12	11	12
Scotland	25	17	40	46	13	13	21	22

Table 1.3 Regional factors and voting behaviour (%)

- **Attitudes towards competence of party leaders.** Polls indicate that this is an important factor in voting behaviour. An important factor in Conservative victories up to 1992 was that they were seen as more competent to manage the country (and particularly the economy) than Labour. However, as a result of major economic problems faced by the Conservatives after 1992, their internal divisions over Europe and their identification with 'sleaze', Labour was seen as more competent in 1997.
- **Leadership.** With the media's increasing focus on party leaders, an important factor is voters' attitudes towards the leaders, their competence and personality, and the way in which their parties project them. In 1992 John Major was seen as a more competent leader than Neil Kinnock in polls taken when people left the polling station (exit polls) and he won. Similarly, in 1997 Tony Blair was seen as a much more competent leader than Major, and won.

B Other influences on voting behaviour

THE MEDIA

There is no agreement among experts about how much influence the media can have either on voting behaviour or in what areas. A number of pieces of evidence are relevant:

- Most people in the UK read a newspaper. In 1992 the majority of newspapers supported the Conservatives and they won. In 1997 the majority of newspapers supported Labour and they won.
- In the late 1980s and early 1990s the general tenor of the press was critical of Labour and the image presented was still that Labour was a radical and divided party. In the final week of the 1992 election campaign, the media switched attention away from health and education issues (which favoured

Labour) to taxation, which favoured the Conservatives. In spite of the economy being in poor condition, the Conservatives won in 1992.

- After the economic crisis of 1992 the media became increasingly hostile to the Conservatives, and were particularly critical of the government's competence. In the run-up to the 1997 election the media focused on 'sleaze' and Europe, closely followed by education and health, and these were issues that showed the Conservative government in a poor light.

- It is also argued that what the media choose *not* to mention can be important. For example, in 1997 the healthy state of the economy, with falling unemployment and inflation, received little mention. Some of the more radical ideas of Labour, particularly on the constitution, also received little attention in the media.

- Experts argue that the way in which Labour was presented in 1997 as 'fresh and energetic' compared with the 'tired and divided' Conservatives was important. The media consistently emphasised that 'New' Labour had given up its old socialist policies.

OPINION POLLS

Analysts disagree about how much influence opinion polls have on elections. In France they are banned in the weeks before an election because it is felt they have a damaging influence on voting behaviour. Some argue that polls might keep potential supporters at home because, if they see the party they support ahead in the polls, they think there is no need for them to vote. In contrast, some voters might be so dispirited at seeing their party 'losing' that they also stay at home. Others argue that polls can create a bandwagon effect, with some voters seeing one party ahead and voting for it in order to be on the winning side.

> Polls are seen too often as election forecasts, when they really should be seen as voting intentions on the day they are taken. They are not good guides to the final outcome, but they are the best that politicians and the media have.

The polls on the whole predicted incorrectly in 1992, but the polling organisations subsequently made changes in their methods of consulting people, and were more accurate in 1997. Exit polls, taken from voters after they have voted, are seen as much more reliable than polls taken before the election.

TACTICAL VOTING

This is a product of the election system currently used in British general elections. It means that a voter does not vote for the party he or she really prefers, knowing that it will not win in that seat, but votes for another party in order to keep out a party the voter particularly dislikes. This was seen as an important factor in some of Labour's successes in 1997, and also helped the Liberal Democrats to win more seats in 1997, even though their overall share of the vote dropped. For example, if the previous result of an election was Conservatives 25,000, Labour 21,000, Liberal Democrats 7,000, a Liberal Democrat voter who particularly disliked the Conservatives might well vote Labour to keep the Conservatives out.

THE INFLUENCE OF THE CAMPAIGNS

Again, experts disagree about how many voters have not made up their minds before the start of the campaign, which usually lasts 3 weeks. Nor is there any agreement about the actual impact of a campaign. Some argue that Labour's campaign of 1992 actually alienated voters because it was overconfident and 'triumphalist'. Others argue that its brilliantly slick and carefully managed campaign of 1997 was critical to its success, and showed Labour to be competent and efficient, in contrast to the Conservatives. On the other hand, some people argue that the campaign only added marginally to Labour's victory in 1997 — it was going to win anyway.

FACTORS AFFECTING TURNOUT IN ELECTIONS

On average about 75% of those entitled to vote actually 'turn out' in general elections. The turnout is much lower in local elections. It dropped to 71% in 1997 and then to 59% in 2001 — the lowest since 1918. An increasing number of people, particularly those between 18 and 25, are not even bothering to register to vote. Various reasons are put forward for the 41% who were entitled to vote, but did not in 1997:

- young people are more mobile and do not feel involved in the community they live in
- simple apathy
- refusing to vote on principle, as they feel alienated from the whole system
- party dealignment — the decreasing identification with a major party
- many voters believed Labour would win easily, so there was no need for them to vote
- too long an election campaign (the campaign of 1997 was much longer than usual) — the voters get bored
- similarity of policy between the parties — quite a contrast with 1983, for example, when there was a great policy divide between Labour and Conservatives
- voters who had always supported one party getting angry with that party. Labour had moved to the 'right' in 1997, and some argue that many of its traditional supporters felt it was not socialist enough, and stayed at home. It is also argued that many Conservative supporters were alienated from their party in 1997 because of its divisions on Europe and accusations of 'sleaze', and also stayed at home.

The general election of 2001

In contrast to previous elections, where a huge amount has been written, many discussions have been held and detailed data are available on the voters, at the time of writing (August 2001) the election of 2001 has so far produced limited debate and information. However, the following key points should be made:

POSSIBLE REASONS FOR LABOUR'S VICTORY

- Opinion polls had consistently predicted victory since 1997. Labour was expected to win. This may have deterred possible Conservative voters from turning out to vote.
- Tony Blair had avoided giving any sign of 'Old Labour' policies of 'tax and spend' reappearing.
- Labour conducted a good campaign and the Conservatives a poor one. The Conservatives might have chosen the wrong agenda (e.g. the euro and asylum

seekers). The press was invariably hostile to, and critical of, the Conservative campaign. Conservative organisation during the campaign was poor, and the press highlighted this. The potential Labour 'disasters' during the campaign, such as John Prescott's infamous punch at a protestor who had thrown an egg and the attacks on Tony Blair for health service failings, generally received gentle treatment from the media. Does this suggest good spin-doctoring? The Liberal Democrats improved their position considerably during the campaign, going from about 12% to 19%, which damaged the Conservatives. The current wisdom on campaigns is that they *can* matter, but no one is sure if they *do*.

- Radio and television are expected to remain impartial, but some critics argue that New Labour's spin-doctors are so good at manipulating them that Labour received highly favourable treatment of such disasters as the Prescott punch. Newspapers were overwhelmingly supportive of Labour — the Murdoch press in particular. Again there is debate among experts about the extent of media influence. The present consensus is that it was important to Labour's victory, but no one is sure exactly how important.

- Labour chose to debate and focus on the issues that were most important to the electorate. Polls indicate that voters saw health and education as the two most important issues and Labour ranked them first and third in the degree of emphasis it gave them in the manifesto and the campaign. The Conservatives ranked them fourth and fifth, and focused the bulk of their campaign on Europe, which the public ranked only tenth. Commentators saw this as a serious error of judgement on the part of Conservative leader William Hague and a key reason why he resigned after losing the election.

- Some commentators see management of the economy as critical to Labour's victory. Gordon Brown was seen as a 'safe pair of hands' by the affluent voters in London and the southeast who swung to Labour in 1997 and stayed loyal in 2001. Some commentators have reservations about this view, arguing that the Conservatives stayed in power in 1992 even though the economy was in a bad way, and lost power in 1997 at a time when the economy was exceptionally healthy. Some argue that the media chose not to emphasise Ken Clarke's economic success of 1992–97 during the 1997 campaign, but kept the focus on the 'Black Wednesday' disaster of 1992. It might be argued that voters did not see the economy as an 'issue' in 2001. They felt comfortable with Gordon Brown and seemed aware that inflation, interest rates and unemployment were well down on 1997.

- Tony Blair managed to adapt his policies to keep the 'core' Labour voters while continuing to appeal to 'middle England'. The Conservatives and Liberal Democrats made no impact on Labour's traditional support.

- New Labour had clearly captured the centre ground of British politics. As one commentator put it, 'Blair has become the least worst choice of middle England.'

- Labour benefited hugely from the structure of the electoral system (see Unit 2). Labour's vote is geographically concentrated in such a way as to gain maximum benefit from the first-past-the-post system. It is doubtful that there will be much support for proportional representation from Labour in the next few years. The electoral system also damaged the Conservatives quite significantly.

- Both the public and the media felt it was appropriate to 'give Labour another chance'.

- The electorate's main concern was to get better public services, and the voters felt that Labour was more likely to deliver on these matters. Certainly the Labour manifesto and campaign had greater focus on public services.
- The Liberal Democrats took even more seats, and these came from the Conservatives.
- The SNP vote was down in Scotland, which was beneficial to Labour as the Nationalists were its principal opponents there.
- The Labour vote held up well in traditional Labour areas, although fewer voters actually voted for it. In the north, 5 million people voted Labour while only 2.4 million voted Conservative. In the traditionally Conservative south, both Labour and the Conservatives received 6 million votes.
- Labour continued to grow in traditionally Conservative suburbia.
- Labour lost a few 'core voters' who may have stayed at home (or voted BNP in some cases), but it gained middle-class voters. The Conservatives still received 44% of the vote among the professional and managerial classes compared to Labour's 37%, but Labour got over 50% of the vote in all other classes. Labour had become much more socially inclusive than the Conservatives.
- Labour benefited from the agenda that the media had set for the election. The basic question posed to the public was 'Is Labour fit for another term?' and the recommended answer was very much 'yes'. The way in which the Conservatives were portrayed, even by radio and television that were supposed to be impartial, was that they were not fit to govern.
- Labour captured the public mood much better than the Conservatives did. The public wished to be led from the left of centre (but not too far left). Conservative promises to reduce taxation, which many felt would lead to a reduction in the quality of public services, simply were not liked by the electorate. It is worth noting that the Liberal Democrats, pledging to increase taxes to fund better public services, did well in former Conservative seats. The Conservatives simply failed to grasp what the electorate felt.

KEY STATISTICS FROM THE 2001 GENERAL ELECTION

Issue	Public opinion rank	Labour rank	Conservative rank	Lib Dem rank
Health	1	1	4	3
Education	2	3	5	2
Law and order	3	7	6	9
Pensions	4	15	11	6
Tax	5	4	2	1
Transport	6	10	14	11
Economy	7	5	7	8
Unemployment	8	18	27	29
Immigration/asylum	9	12	3	10
Europe	10	2	1	5

Source: MORI poll published in *The Times,* 7 June 2001

Table 1.4 The issue agenda

	Conservative	Labour	Liberal Democrat
Middle class (AB)	39	30	25
Lower middle class (C1)	36	38	20
Skilled working class (C2)	29	49	15
Unskilled working class (DE)	24	55	13
Source: MORI, 20 July 2001			

Table 1.5 Voting by class (%)

	Conservative	Labour	Liberal Democrat
18–24	27	41	24
25–34	24	51	19
35–44	28	45	19
45–54	32	41	20
55–64	39	37	17
65+	40	39	17
Source: MORI, 20 July 2001			

Table 1.6 Voting by age (%)

	Conservative	Labour
Men	32	42
Women	33	42
Source: MORI, 20 July 2001		

Table 1.7 Voting by gender (%)

	Labour	Conservative	Liberal Democrat
Scotland	44	16	16
Wales	62	21	14
North	56	25	17
Yorkshire and Humberside	49	30	17
North West	52	28	17
West Midlands	43	35	15
East Midlands	45	37	15
East Anglia	36	42	19
South East	32	43	22
London	47	31	18
South West	26	31	39
Source: MORI, 20 July 2001			

Table 1.8 Voting by region (%)

This is a major topic for all three examination boards. AQA and OCR both have a unit where roughly 50% of the content deals with this topic; in Edexcel the topic forms an important part of two units. The issue of electoral reform must be known in considerable detail and there is a very strong case for learning statistics from the past two or three elections, as well as the results of elections for the EU and the new Scottish Parliament and the assemblies.

Key questions

What are the merits and demerits of the British electoral system?

What are the arguments for and against bringing in a system of PR for British general elections?

Should the UK have more referendums?

What are the key differences between the differing voting systems in the UK?

Who has the right to vote in the UK? Who should have the right to vote?

A The electoral system in the UK

A basic outline knowledge of the history of the right to vote is needed.

THE HISTORY OF BRITISH ELECTIONS

Electing MPs for parliament goes back many hundreds of years. The first step towards giving all adults the right to vote was made in 1832, when disenfranchised (voteless) middle-class men threatened revolution unless the aristocracy gave them the vote. This meant that the electorate (those with the right to vote) went up from 2% to 7% of the adult population. Voting was gradually extended in the nineteenth century to better-off working-class men in 1867 and 1884. Voting was done in secret (1872) and honestly (1883/1885). In 1918 women under 30 and all males got the vote. Women over 21 got the vote in 1928 and the age of voting was dropped to 18 in 1969.

THE FRANCHISE IN THE UK

Now about 99% of the population over the age of 18 are allowed to vote. In the nineteenth century, only property owners were able to vote. Now the requirement is to be a British citizen who has registered and is on the **electoral register** (list of voters). Until 1949 some people had two votes, if they were graduates or owned a business in a different **constituency** (area which sends MPs to parliament) from the one in which they lived. Now every voter has only one vote per election. Members of the House of Lords, the royal family, those certified insane and those in prison may not vote. Voting is not compulsory, as it is in some countries.

The issue of whether special qualifications or skills are needed to be an MP is a very likely question.

WHO CAN BE A PARLIAMENTARY CANDIDATE?

To stand for parliament, you have to be over 21 and a British citizen. No other qualifications, including educational ones, are needed. Criminals convicted of serious crimes, bankrupts, clergy and some officials, such as judges, may not stand as MPs. There are very tight restrictions (dating back to 1883) on how much can be spent on an election. Several elected MPs had legal proceedings started against them in 1997 for failing to observe the rules about spending, and one was convicted.

PRINCIPLES OF ELECTIONS IN THE UK

Think carefully about what ought to be the underlying principles of an electoral system.

- What should an electoral system be trying to achieve?
- Should it produce a strong government?
- Should the aim be to have one party with a majority of the seats in Parliament?
- Should it be to produce strong leadership?
- Should it reflect as accurately as possible the views and opinions of the public?
- Should the aim be to avoid **coalition** government (government by more than one party)?

> Before starting to criticise or praise the system used for general elections in the UK, think about what the objectives of the British system should be.

THE TIMING OF GENERAL ELECTIONS

The Parliament Act of 1911 states that a general election must be held at least every five years. However, prime ministers can hold an election earlier by asking the monarch to agree to one (there is a convention that the monarch always agrees) if they think they have a good chance of winning. In times of crisis, it is possible to postpone an election — this happened in 1915 and 1940, during the two world wars. However, this can only be done if the House of Lords agrees — and it is the only issue over which the Lords have a full veto. Tony Blair held his most recent election in June 2001, nearly a year before he had to. Some feel that this gives the prime minister too much influence over the result, since he or she can choose the time most favourable to the prime minister's own party.

> An issue that needs careful thought is whether the UK ought to have a fixed period between elections, as in the USA, or whether it is right in a democracy to leave the decision to the prime minister.

BY-ELECTIONS

By-elections occur when there is a single vacancy in one constituency: for example, when an MP dies. The same rules apply as with general elections, but there is usually great media interest and a much higher level of spending by each party is allowed. By-elections can be seen as important ways of gauging public opinion between general elections. Unusually, Tony Blair's government between 1997 and 2001 did quite well in by-elections, although in many cases the number of Labour voters fell.

> By-elections are often seen by parties as important tests of public opinion.

LOCAL ELECTIONS

These are fixed term, taking place every 4 years. The same rules about who may be a candidate apply in local elections as in general elections. Like general elections, local elections are usually conducted on party lines, but the turnout is much lower than is the case with general elections: usually less than a third of the electorate votes. In some local elections every councillor is up for re-election every fourth year, while in others some are elected each year — but still for a four-year term.

> The main difference between local and general elections is that the former are set at regular intervals.

EUROPEAN ELECTIONS

The UK is entitled to send 87 MEPs (Members of the European Parliament) to the European Parliament. This number may change if the EU is enlarged. There are considerable differences between the way in which MEPs and MPs are elected. The system used for European elections is a type of proportional representation called the **closed-list** system. You need to know this system well, and the main differences between it and the system used in general elections in the UK. The main features of the system are as follows:

- It is similar to the system used in other EU countries.
- Voters choose parties and not candidates on their ballot papers.
- Voters vote regionally and not in individual constituencies.
- The UK is divided into 12 regions, and each region, such as the South East, is given about one MEP per 500,000 voters. The South East, for example, gets 11 MEPs.
- If a party gets 50% of the vote in a region that has four MEPs allocated, it will get two of those seats, and they will be the first two candidates named on the party's list of candidates for that region.
- There are similar rules about deposits and spending as with British elections.

Note how the parties performed in the European elections of 1999.

ELECTIONS FOR THE SCOTTISH PARLIAMENT

This is very different from the system used for British general elections.

- There are 129 MSPs (Members of the Scottish Parliament).
- There are 73 constituencies.
- Each voter has two votes: one for a constituency MSP and one for a party.
- One MSP is elected from each constituency using the simple plurality system used in British general elections.
- A further 56 MSPs are chosen using a closed-list system very similar to the one described above for European elections — this is where the second vote is used.
- Scotland is divided into eight regions, which are the same as the 'Euroregions'. Each region has 7 MSPs and they are elected on a proportional basis. If a party wins 60% of the vote in a region, then it will get four of the seven MSP seats allocated to that region.

The Conservatives gained no seats in the constituencies, even though they had more than 20% of the vote, but they gained seats in the Scottish Parliament through the closed-list system in the regions (see Table 2.1).

	Constituency contests		Regional lists		
	Share of vote	Seats won	Share of vote	Seats won	Total no. of seats won
Conservative	16%	0	15%	18	18
Labour	39%	53	34%	3	56
Liberal Democrat	14%	12	12%	5	17
SNP	29%	7	27%	28	35

Table 2.1 The results of the elections to the Scottish Parliament, 1999

Note the very considerable variations between the share of the vote and the seats won under the two different systems. Note also that it has produced a coalition government in Scotland.

THE WELSH ASSEMBLY ELECTIONS

The Welsh system is virtually identical to the Scottish system.
- The simple plurality system is used in the 40 'ordinary' constituencies.
- A further 20 members are elected — using closed party lists — from the five regions, which are the same as European constituencies.

THE ELECTORAL SYSTEM IN NORTHERN IRELAND

One reason for the very different electoral system in Northern Ireland is that different objectives were sought: for example, to ensure that Roman Catholic voters were properly represented.

The electoral history of Northern Ireland is very different from the rest of the UK. There had been many concerns about the extent to which constituency boundaries had been **gerrymandered** (drawn in such a way as to ensure that one type of candidate was elected) and about the accuracy of the voter lists. (The old saying 'vote early and vote often' comes from Northern Ireland, and investigations in the 1970s revealed that a very large number of dead people had managed to vote as well.) The system used is a proportional representation system.

B The first-past-the-post system

The proper name for the system used in British general elections is the **simple plurality system**. However, it is frequently called the **first-past-the-post (FPTP) system**. The UK is divided up into just over 650 single-member constituencies, each sending one MP to parliament. Regardless of how many candidates stand in a constituency, the candidate with the greatest number of votes is the winner, even if the majority of those who voted did not vote for the winner. Those who wish to stand as candidates must put down a deposit of £500, which is returned if the candidate gets more than 5% of the votes cast. This is designed to stop too many candidates standing. There are very strict rules about how much money each candidate can spend.

ADVANTAGES OF FIRST PAST THE POST

The merits of this system (really designed in 1885 by the Conservatives and Liberals to ensure that radical parties would not win any seats) are as follows:
- It is simple to operate and understand.
- The results are easily understood.
- It tends to give the winning party a larger proportion of the total seats than its proportion of the votes. The largest party usually has a clear majority, which avoids the need for coalition governments, where two or more parties have to join together to form a government. Coalitions can involve a lot of negotiating and 'deals' before a government can be formed. This happened in Scotland after the first elections for the Scottish Parliament.
- Each constituency gets an MP who has to look after the interests of that constituency and its inhabitants. There is a strong local link between the MP and his or her constituency.

- It usually produces a strong government (but look at 1974 elections) and the public seems comfortable with it.

DISADVANTAGES OF FIRST PAST THE POST

- Too often a majority of the voters in a constituency vote against the winner. This could be seen as undemocratic.
- Any government can represent only a minority of the voters. Look at the figures for 1997.
- It is possible for the majority of the voters to vote for one party, while another party actually gets more seats and therefore wins the election. This happened in both 1951 and 1974.
- It can lead to 'safe' seats, where one party always wins a seat in a particular constituency. This is not good for democracy.
- A few voters changing their minds in a few marginal seats can change a government. For example, look at the figures for 1974.
- It can lead to a situation such as in Scotland in 1997, when nearly 20% of the electorate voted for one party (the Conservatives) and yet they did not win a single seat in parliament for that country.
- Voters only have one vote. What happens if they like the candidate for one party, but not most of the ideas that the candidate's party represents?

In the 2001 general election, Labour had a majority of 167 seats.

Party	No. of votes	% of votes cast	Seats won
Labour	10.7 million	42	413
Conservative	8.4 million	33	166
Liberal Democrat	4.8 million	19	52

Table 2.2 First past the post in practice: general election, 2001

In Tables 2.2 and 2.3, look at the relationship between votes cast and seats won, particularly for the Conservatives and Liberal Democrats. Note also that the *majority* of those who voted (13.2 million) did not vote for the winners.

Party	% of vote	% of seats in Parliament
Labour	42	64
Conservative	33	26
Liberal Democrat	19	8

Table 2.3 Votes and seats in Great Britain: general election, 2001

The Liberal Democrats lost votes in the 2001 election, their vote falling from 5.2 million in 1997 to 4.8 million in 2001 — but their number of seats went up from 44 to 52.

Party	Share of the vote	Seats won at Westminster
Labour	44%	56
Conservative	16%	1
Liberal Democrat	16%	10
SNP	20%	5

Table 2.4 Votes and seats in Scotland: general election, 2001

A clear picture of the merits and demerits of the British electoral system is vital, and you need to know some statistics to back up the points you make.

Tactical voting has become increasingly important in general elections.

It is easy to find other statistics from the 2001 general election that can be used to point out the unfairness of the British electoral system. For example, in Scotland the relationship between seats and votes cast was as shown in Table 2.4.

It is possible that the Scottish results will weaken the Conservative Party's opposition to proportional representation.

TACTICAL VOTING

Another perceived failing of the first-past-the-post system is that it can lead to tactical voting. This occurs when voters in a constituency who happen to support party A realise that there is no chance of their favoured party winning, so they vote for party B in order to try and stop the candidate for party C winning. They dislike party C most, so they vote for a party they don't dislike as much, but don't really prefer, as the lesser of two evils. One of the reasons why both Labour and the Liberal Democrats did so well in 1997 and 2001 was because of tactical voting: many Liberals voted Labour in some seats to keep out the Conservatives, while in other constituencies, Labour voters backed Liberals also to keep out the Conservatives.

C Other electoral systems

You need to have a reasonable working knowledge of other types of electoral system, particularly those in use in other nations of the EU. There are two broad types:
- proportional electoral systems
- majoritarian electoral systems

PROPORTIONAL SYSTEMS

The main proportional systems are as follows:
- **The list system.** This is used in EU countries like Belgium and Spain. Quite simply it means that if a party gets 45% of the votes cast, it gets 45% of the seats in parliament. The constituencies tend to be very large, with as many as 20 MPs being elected for each. It is mathematically very correct, but it is criticised for giving a lot of power to the parties themselves, which decide the candidates on their lists. Also it does not produce MPs with a strong constituency link.

This is the system that most advocates of electoral reform in the UK would like to produce.

- **The single transferable vote (STV) system.** Under this system a country is divided into multi-member constituencies: in Ireland, for example, they are county-sized, each returning several MPs to parliament. Five is a common number. The voter has five votes in a five-member constituency, and lists his or her votes in order of preference. If a candidate gets more than 20% of first preference votes, he or she is elected. Once a candidate gets more than 20% of the votes cast, the remainder of his or her votes are transferred to the voters' second choices. To be elected, a candidate has to get a quota and the quota is worked out by using the **Droop formula**:

$$\text{quota} = \frac{\text{total number of votes cast} + 1}{\text{number of seats in the constituency} + 1}$$

Parties tend to take a lot of care in selecting candidates under this system in order to give the electorate plenty of choice: for example, there are more women candidates. The constituency link is retained, the voter gets more choice and the number of seats won by parties tends to reflect the proportions of the vote they received nationally. Voters tend to vote for candidates and not parties, and it is in the interest of all parties to work hard at election time to educate the voters about the merits of their candidates. In some countries it produces a majority government; in others it does not. It is worth noting that there is no evidence that it produces political instability.

- **The additional member system (AMS).** This is the system adopted for elections to the Scottish Parliament, where voters have two votes, one for a constituency MP and one for a party. (See p.15 for full details.)

ADVANTAGES OF PROPORTIONAL REPRESENTATION

- It does not cause 'wasted' votes. A wasted vote can occur in a constituency when one party has a huge majority, usually over 20,000, and the wasted vote goes to the losing party. Wasted votes can account for as many as 70% of the total in some areas. Under PR all votes count.
- There are fewer safe seats. In 1983 the Conservatives' vote dropped but they increased their seats. It took just 35,000 Conservative votes to produce one Conservative MP, while it took over 300,000 Liberal voters to produce a Liberal MP. This does not happen under PR.
- The government, which may be a coalition, represents a majority of the voters, and not a minority as under first past the post. 17.5% of the voters who voted Conservative in Scotland in 1997 did not have a single MP to represent their views in Parliament. Under PR this would not happen.
- It tends to produce a more representative group of MPs, as in Ireland.
- It avoids the situation where a few marginal seats control the whole result.
- Parties whose vote is geographically scattered gain seats, whereas under first past the post the Conservatives in Scotland or in Durham cannot achieve representation.

DISADVANTAGES OF PROPORTIONAL REPRESENTATION

- The link between constituents and their MP may be lost.
- It might lead to constant coalition governments, with minority parties holding the balance between two much larger ones, and thus wielding too much influence. It might be argued that this happened in the UK between 1976 and 1979, when Labour had no majority in parliament and was dependent on a few Liberal MPs to stay in power.
- Accountability might be lost, with a small group in a coalition dictating policy, but the larger party having to take responsibility.
- The parties that make up a coalition might make secret 'deals' without the voters knowing.

MAJORITARIAN SYSTEMS

In addition to the British first-past-the-post system there are three other types of majoritarian system:

- **The two-ballot or second ballot system.** This is mainly used in France.

The merits and demerits of PR are a very likely focus for a question. Candidates must be prepared to argue this issue out in depth, and bring in statistics from both the UK and other EU countries to back up their points.

If a candidate wins more than 50% of the vote, he or she is elected. If no candidate gets more than half of the votes, the weaker candidates withdraw and there is a second election in which voters can reconsider their vote. The process continues until one candidate has over 50% of the vote.

- **The alternative vote (AV) system.** This happens in single-member constituencies with voters listing candidates in order of preference. The candidate with the fewest first preferences is eliminated and this continues until one candidate has a majority.
- **The supplementary vote** (once supported by the Labour Party). Here a voter has just two preferences. If no candidate gets 50% of the vote, all but the top two candidates are withdrawn and their second choices are distributed.

Again the merits and demerits of majoritarian systems need to be known. Be prepared to contrast them with the advantages and disadvantages of PR.

ADVANTAGES OF MAJORITARIAN SYSTEMS
- They keep the link between constituents and their MP.
- The winner (eventually) gets more than 50% of the vote.
- They tend to produce strong governments with majorities.
- They are easy to understand.
- There are no wasted votes.

DISADVANTAGES OF MAJORITARIAN SYSTEMS
- They can encourage electoral pacts between parties to damage a third, as parties tend to recommend that their voters put the other favoured party as second choice.
- They tend to favour centre parties.

ELECTION STATISTICS
It has been argued, based on extensive polling, that if the British general election of 1997 had been conducted under a different electoral system, the results would have been as shown in Table 2.5.

	FPTP	List	AV	STV	AMS	Supp. vote
Conservative	165	202	110	144	203	110
Labour	419	285	436	342	303	436
Liberal Democrat	46	110	84	131	115	84

Table 2.5 Number of seats which might have been won in 1997 under different electoral systems

The Liberal Democrats have naturally always been keen on electoral reform, while Labour has become much less enthusiastic. It is becoming clear now that the Conservative Party, always very strong opponents of electoral reform, might have most to gain after the 2001 election from moving to a reformed electoral system.

D Referendums

The recent growth in the use of referendums is of major constitutional significance — this is now a major AS topic.

THE HISTORY OF REFERENDUMS IN THE UK

A referendum is a vote on a single issue: for example, whether or not the voter wishes the UK to stay in the EU. Until recent years there was no tradition of holding referendums in the UK. Other countries tend to have them when a major constitutional change is being considered, and the UK is moving in a similar direction.

You should know about the following referendums:

- **Northern Ireland, 1973.** This referendum was called in the hope of finding a solution to the growing violence in Northern Ireland. Voters in Northern Ireland only were asked whether they wished Northern Ireland to remain in the UK. The result was very much in favour, but large sections of the population refused to vote in the referendum, so it had limited impact. The British government did not agree to be bound by its findings.
- **Membership of the EU, 1975.** Leading a government badly divided over membership of the EU (then known as the European Economic Community), Labour prime minister Harold Wilson called for the first major nation-wide referendum on whether the UK should remain a member. The verdict was that it should. The referendum ended party disunity on the matter — for a while. Wilson was careful not to let the result be binding. It is unlikely that he (always a supporter of the EU) would have called for the referendum if he had thought he might lose it. There was a strong feeling among the opponents of the EU that the government propaganda machine was used unfairly to persuade people to vote to stay in. There was also criticism that the way in which the question was worded was designed to produce an answer in favour of staying in the EU.
- **Devolution for Scotland and Wales, 1979.** Partly as the price for keeping the Liberals' support for his minority Labour government, prime minister James Callaghan agreed to have a referendum in Scotland and Wales (the English were not consulted) on whether there should be devolution for Scotland and Wales. There was limited support in Wales for it, and although the majority of those who voted for it in Scotland were in favour, the government decided that as those who voted in favour were less than 40% of the total electorate, devolution had, in effect, been defeated. Even then the government had not agreed to be bound by the result. As a result, referendums became rather discredited in the eyes of the public. Again it was clear that the government would not have embarked on the referendum unless it had been fairly sure that devolution would not win.
- **Devolution for Scotland and Wales, 1997.** Voters in Scotland were asked two questions. The first was whether they wanted a Scottish Parliament and the second was whether they wanted the Scottish Parliament to have tax-varying powers. On both issues they voted 'yes'. The Welsh were asked only one question about limited devolution. This time the government did agree to be bound by the results, and devolution has subsequently gone through. Here the government supported the measures, which had been in the Labour manifesto. But Tony Blair's government was anxious not to be seen as pushing through

a huge constitutional change without consultation, just by using its huge parliamentary majority. The fact that Labour dominates the Scottish Parliament might be noted.

- **Northern Ireland, 1998.** This had two purposes: first, to get support for the Northern Ireland peace process; and second, to get endorsement for devolved powers to Northern Ireland and end the direct rule of Northern Ireland from London. As many political leaders in Northern Ireland opposed the peace process, the referendum was seen as an appeal by the British (and Irish) government over the heads of the politicians and paramilitary leaders to the people. With a high turnout and more than a two-thirds majority in favour, this put real pressure on the political leaders of Northern Ireland to accept the Good Friday Agreement.

- **The mayor of London, 1998.** This referendum asked the people of London if they wanted an elected mayor with powers to deal with certain aspects of London as a whole, such as transport. The result was positive, but the turnout was very low.

THE CASE FOR REFERENDUMS

It is very likely that you will be asked to weigh up the cases for and against referendums.

- They are highly democratic.
- They involve citizens in major issues that affect their whole lives.
- They encourage participation.
- They give a government consent for a specific action.
- They can be used to overcome obstacles, such as happened in Northern Ireland in 1998.
- They can end controversy on highly divisive issues.

THE CASE AGAINST REFERENDUMS

- They go totally against the UK's traditional system of representative democracy, where elected representatives in parliament make major decisions after debating all the relevant issues.
- Governments sometimes only hold them when they are sure they will win.
- The wording of the questions could be misleading, as was argued in the 1975 referendum.
- Some issues are highly complex, such as whether to join the euro, and to make a good decision on a highly sophisticated topic requires a degree of expert knowledge, which many of the electorate will not possess.
- There is a risk that a decision, such as the reintroduction of capital punishment, might be forced on a government that thinks it is totally wrong.
- There is a risk that majorities will use referendums to impose restrictions on minorities.

E Key terms and concepts

Boundary Commission An independent body charged with redrawing constituency boundaries to compensate for the increase/decrease in population for an area. It is a difficult task that requires impartiality, as the way in which boundaries are drawn on the map can affect whether a seat is won or lost by a party at election time.

Constituency A geographical area that has the right to send one MP to parliament. There are usually about 70,000 voters in each constituency in the UK.

Democracy A system of government based on the participation of all qualified citizens in decision making — and one where the right to vote is fundamental to the system.

Electorate All those entitled to vote. Note that in 2001, 59% of the electorate voted in the UK.

Franchise The right to vote.

Mandate Basically 'permission'. When a party wins an election and forms a government, it feels that it now has the permission of the electorate to put into practice the promises it made in its manifesto.

Proportional representation A system of voting which seeks to ensure that there is a direct mathematical relationship between the number of votes cast and the number of seats gained in an election.

Referendum An opportunity for the electorate to vote on one single issue.

Tactical voting When a voter does not vote for his or her first preference party (which may not stand a chance of winning a seat), but votes for another party in order to keep out a third party that the voter particularly dislikes.

Naturally this is a central topic for all three examination boards. The development of the office should be known, and above all you should be familiar with the power and influence of the modern prime minister. The examiners will expect a reasonably good working knowledge of prime ministers from 1979 onwards, and candidates should be able to compare, say, Margaret Thatcher with Tony Blair. Lots of examples of what prime ministers have or have not been able to do need to be known. Avoid any personal comments when writing about the topic.

Key questions

What are the powers of the prime minister?

What are the limits to the prime minister's powers?

Has the prime minister become too powerful?

In what ways has the office of prime minister changed in recent years?

Who has power within the executive?

A Evolution of the office of prime minister

There are plenty of examples before the eighteenth century of British monarchs having one minister whom they relied on above all others, and to whom they often delegated substantial power. In the sixteenth century Queen Elizabeth I allowed William Cecil huge influence, but she was perfectly capable of ignoring his advice and ordering him to follow her instructions.

Like all vital parts of the British political system, the office of prime minister simply emerged over the course of time.

DEVELOPMENT OF THE OFFICE IN THE EIGHTEENTH CENTURY

It was not until the early eighteenth century that the office of prime minister emerged in the United Kingdom. No law was passed saying that there would be a prime minister. The office emerged because there was a need for it, and everyone accepted the development of the office, so it became part of the British constitution. It became a convention.

The first prime minister was Robert Walpole. He emerged as the prime minister, as opposed to being a minister like any other, for the following reasons:

- He had the confidence of the king — he was trusted by the king to act on his behalf.
- He could manage the House of Commons and get necessary laws passed.
- He had the confidence of many Members of Parliament — he was trusted by them.
- He could manage a team of ministers, known as the cabinet.
- He had proved to be a competent administrator and was good at managing the economy.

- He had the ability to produce the policies necessary to ensure that the country was properly defended and administered.

By the time Walpole left office in 1742, having lost the confidence of the House of Commons, the broad powers of the office of prime minister were accepted by all, and had become part of the constitution. Those powers were:

- the control of all major appointments, not only of ministers and civil servants, but also of such figures as the key judges, generals and bishops
- the setting of the nation's agenda, deciding what policy might be, both domestic and foreign, and dominating parliament and the law-making process

The main powers — and limitations — of the office of prime minister were in place by 1800.

The limitations of the office were also recognised: the prime minister needed the confidence of the House of Commons and the support of the cabinet.

Pitt the Younger, prime minister in the last years of the eighteenth and the first years of the nineteenth century, took all the key decisions while directing the war against Napoleon, and also played the dominant role in deciding how the economy might be reformed and administered. Many may have disagreed with his policies, but no one contested his right to be able to push those policies through.

DEVELOPMENT OF THE OFFICE IN THE NINETEENTH AND TWENTIETH CENTURIES

Tony Blair holds an office not dissimilar in power and influence to that held by Pitt in 1800, and Pitt also lived in Downing Street. The changes taking place in the nineteenth and twentieth centuries were relatively minor. The role of party leader was added in the nineteenth century, as modern political parties emerged. Some argue that although being a party leader can help a prime minister dominate the policy-making process, party issues can also weaken and limit a prime minister. The right of the prime minister to decide the date of general elections also began in the nineteenth century, while the monarch's ability to influence the choice of ministers and then the prime minister was lost in 1821 and 1834–35 respectively.

With the arrival of total war in the twentieth century, wartime prime ministers such as Lloyd George and Churchill had to take on huge additional powers, e.g. total control of the workforce and the economy, in order to win those wars.

The prime minister's official title — it was the one that Walpole held.

Officially prime ministers were not supposed to have the sort of power they actually had.

OFFICIAL RECOGNITION OF THE OFFICE OF PRIME MINISTER

Everyone knew there was a 'prime' minister, and the holders of the office of 'first lord of the treasury' were always called prime minister. However, it was one of the 'constitutional works of authority', written by Walter Bagehot in the 1860s, which first discussed the office of prime minister in depth.

Bagehot gave some idea of the power and influence of the prime minister, but he referred to him as 'primus inter pares' which means 'first amongst equals' in Latin. Critics felt that this did not give a true picture, as the prime ministers of the nineteenth century had neither seen themselves in such a light nor behaved in such a way. They had all dominated their cabinets and had played a major part in setting the nation's agenda.

B Sources of the prime minister's power

Whereas the president of the United States has his or her powers clearly listed in the American constitution, the British prime minister's powers come from several different sources.

THE OLD ROYAL PREROGATIVES

Prerogatives were the powers that medieval monarchs had, such as the ability to declare war and to appoint ministers. Over the centuries these powers were gradually transferred from monarchs to prime ministers. Monarchs used to appoint generals; Tony Blair now decides who heads the armed services.

HEAD OF THE EXECUTIVE

The prime minister exercises the role of head of the executive — the principal and final decision-taker in the country. There is an expectation that such a person will provide leadership, initiate policies and broadly influence the direction in which the country is going. It was Margaret Thatcher who, when the Argentinians invaded the Falkland Islands, decided to go to war and take them back.

HEAD OF A POLITICAL PARTY

This gives the prime minister tremendous influence over the making of policy through the party manifesto. If the prime minister's party has a majority in parliament, then the party leader (who is also prime minister) has the ability to put her or his ideas into practice by making them the law of the land. Tony Blair wished to see devolution for Scotland; those ideas went into the 1997 Labour Party manifesto, and when the election was won, Blair's Labour majority in the House of Commons passed devolution for Scotland into law.

Many voters vote for the leader of a party rather than for the party itself or its parliamentary candidates. This enables prime ministers who have won elections to see it as the public approving of them individually and their policies.

Note that many of these sources of power are vague and ill defined.

EMERGENCY POWERS

Not only are specific powers given to the prime minister by act of parliament to enable him to act in an emergency, but there is also an expectation by the public that the prime minister will act decisively in an emergency. For example, there was an expectation that Tony Blair and his government would act to help solve the foot-and-mouth crisis of 2001. The government acted by introducing the compulsory mass 'culling' of animals. People generally expect strong leadership during a crisis, such as the threat of invasion in 1940 and the fuel crisis of 2000.

C The powers of the prime minister

APPOINTMENT AND DISMISSAL OF MINISTERS

This is always seen as the prime minister's most important power. It enables him or her to reward the loyal and to dismiss opponents and rivals. The prime minister can put into key offices, such as the chancellor of the exchequer and the foreign secretary, men and women who share the prime minister's views on the economy and foreign policy. If they are not prepared to follow the prime minister's views, he or she can dismiss them or move them to less important departments. The prime minister can promote ambitious MPs to junior posts in the government, and then promote them into the cabinet when they have proved their competence and loyalty. In 1962 Harold Macmillan demonstrated his power by dismissing 24 ministers in one day.

APPOINTMENT OF CABINET COMMITTEES

Key decisions and policy recommendations are increasingly made by small groups of cabinet ministers working in a cabinet committee. It is the prime minister who decides what issues go to what committee and who sits on these committees of ministers. Again this gives the prime minister tremendous influence. Tony Blair had promised constitutional reform in his manifesto of 1997, but was personally never keen on it; nor did he want radical change. The cabinet committee set up to recommend reform proposals consequently had a majority of quite conservative ministers. The proposals they recommended were not radical.

OTHER APPOINTMENTS

The prime minister also plays an important part in the appointment of many other key officials. He or she will choose the top judges on the advice of the lord chancellor, and also appoint the senior members of the armed services, the bishops of the Church of England and the chairman of governors of the BBC. All of these appointments give the prime minister considerable influence. Tony Blair has also played a part in choosing some of the key ministers in the devolved administrations in Scotland and Wales.

CONTROL OF THE GOVERNMENT AGENDA

Frequently books suggest that a key power of the prime minister is to control the agenda of the cabinet. While it is true that the prime minister has this power, it is not especially important. Major items, such as a bomb explosion in Northern Ireland or a backbench revolt, will often force themselves on to the cabinet's agenda. What is much more important is the prime minister's ability to decide the major priority of the government at that time. For example, if peace in Northern Ireland is the priority, the prime minister might consider taking the following actions:

- giving Northern Ireland the best ministers
- devoting much of the cabinet's time to this issue
- flying to Northern Ireland or the Irish Republic to meet people
- using the status of his office to pressurise people

- adding his presence at key negotiations
- persuading the chancellor of the exchequer to give Northern Ireland more resources (and thereby to deprive someone else of those resources)
- persuading the president of the United States to come over and help
- phoning the Irish prime minister at key moments, etc.

Other important examples in recent years of a prime minister placing great emphasis on a major policy are:

- Margaret Thatcher's focus on privatising many nationalised industries in the 1980s
- John Major's introduction of the Citizen's Charter and the further integration of the UK with the rest of Europe
- Tony Blair's insistence on the economic ideas of New Labour

CONTROL OF THE CIVIL SERVICE

A key development of Mrs Thatcher's premiership was that the prime minister played a vital role in the appointment of the top civil servants who advise ministers and help them in the administration of the country. Although the Labour opposition criticised her at the time for breaking the constitutional 'rules' on this matter, the Labour government has not changed the practice. This ensures not only that ministers are fully loyal to the prime minister, but that many of the top civil servants are too. It was argued that Margaret Thatcher 'politicised' the top civil service by having such an influence over key appointments, but there have certainly been fewer reports in recent years that the civil service has tried to prevent a government carrying out its policies.

CONTROL OF PARLIAMENT

Because Tony Blair has a large majority in the House of Commons, this enables him to ensure that his ideas can become law. He wanted to reform the House of Lords, parliament supported him and the House of Lords has been changed. Two important figures in his cabinet are the leader of the House of Commons and the leader of the House of Lords, and it is their job to ensure that what the prime minister and the government want to be passed through parliament actually is passed. In addition, he appoints the chief whip, who has the responsibility of ensuring that the government's wishes are carried out by having the support of Labour MPs in parliamentary votes and in the standing committees of the House of Commons.

INFLUENCE OVER THE MEDIA

At times, such as during the premiership of John Major, the media can damage the power and influence of the prime minister. However, Tony Blair has proved to be much better at managing the media. He makes full use of the fact that all his actions are reported and his speeches get wide coverage. He insists that the whole of his government 'sings from the same hymn sheet' and he ensures that he gets over the message that he wishes the British people to hear. The prime minister is always news, and he makes full use of that.

ABILITY TO ACT IN AN EMERGENCY

In addition to the powers that are given to the prime minister and his government under the Emergency Powers Act, the public will usually support firm action by a prime minister to deal with emergencies of any type. When Margaret Thatcher wished to stop the miners from blocking fuel supplies, she got extensive public support for her firm actions against the picketing miners. Much the same applied when she decided to go to war with Argentina over the Falklands.

PEERAGES AND HONOURS

In addition to appointing members of the government, the prime minister can reward loyal service by granting a peerage, a knighthood or another honour to his or her supporters. Loyal backbenchers were frequently made knights by Mrs Thatcher, while Tony Blair has placed long-term Labour supporters in the House of Lords.

AIDES TO THE PRIME MINISTER

Various offices exist to help the prime minister carry out his or her duties. The key ones are as follows:

- **Private Office.** This is staffed mainly by civil servants, who are there to ensure that the right information gets to the prime minister, and that his or her wishes are communicated outwards.
- **Press Office.** This is currently run by a very powerful figure, Alastair Campbell, who not only deals with the way in which the prime minister communicates to the public, but also controls media access to the prime minister.
- **Political Unit.** This deals with all Labour Party matters and is how the prime minister communicates with the Labour Party. It is not seen as important.
- **Policy Unit.** This gives the prime minister sources of ideas and policies apart from ministers and their departments. The prime minister might have advisers in areas such as agriculture and foreign policy. They can be very influential. Tony Blair has been criticised for increasing the number of advisers who work directly for him (double the number who worked for Margaret Thatcher) and for giving them much more influence over government policy than has been the case in the past. Previously, prime ministers took advice from civil servants, who were seen as more accountable and 'safer' than the prime minister's own advisers.
- **Political advisers and task forces.** The prime minister also has the ability to set up a group to recommend policy, or to appoint a special adviser in a particular area, such as drugs policy.

VARIABLE FACTORS

Several factors may give a prime minister additional power and influence. Others may reduce that power and influence.

As always in this type of topic, ensure that these main points can be backed up with recent examples.

- **Electoral performance.** Winning the elections of 1979, 1983 and 1987 was a great help to Mrs Thatcher. It showed very clearly to her party that her ideas were popular. However, losing elections can end a prime minister's career abruptly. Look at what happened to John Major in 1997, and Edward Heath in 1974, when he lost two elections in one year.
- **Policy successes.** Mrs Thatcher's prestige increased after the successful Falklands War of 1982, as did John Major's after the Gulf War in the early 1990s. However, making a serious error of judgement can really damage the status of the prime minister. Examples of this are Mrs Thatcher's enthusiasm

for the poll tax, John Major and British membership of the exchange rate mechanism, and Tony Blair's handling of the fuel crisis of 2000.

- **Opinion poll ratings.** John Major suffered badly from poor opinion polls throughout his premiership from 1992 to 1997, while Tony Blair benefited from his good polls between 1997 and 2001.
- **Influence over the cabinet.** Those who have the sheer personality to dominate the cabinet and eliminate possible opponents, such as Mrs Thatcher after 1983, will find fewer obstacles to the exercise of their power. However, between 1979 and 1983 Mrs Thatcher did find it difficult to get her ideas through on Rhodesia and public spending cuts because of cabinet opposition. Tony Blair has found it easy to get his views through as he insists on cabinet obedience.
- **Support in the parliamentary party.** Tony Blair has found it much easier to get his way because most of the time all Labour MPs support him. John Major's power was seriously reduced as he got little support from several of his backbench MPs.
- **Size of parliamentary majority.** Tony Blair has a huge majority in the Commons; his bills become laws easily. John Major frequently had no majority in the Commons, so his bills often did not get through. James Callaghan had no majority between 1977 and 1979 and was dependent on a few Liberals to get any laws through. This seriously weakened his position.
- **Media support or opposition.** John Major and Harold Wilson (1966–70) both had sustained and very hostile media campaigns against them. This encouraged opposition against them at all levels. Tony Blair has had very strong newspaper support since coming into office and this has helped his position. It is worth noting that when there has been strong media criticism of his government's management of an issue, as with old age pensions, his government has responded quickly to limit the criticism.
- **Prime minister's personality.** A strong, domineering and forceful personality will also help. Margaret Thatcher and Tony Blair are examples of this: they insist on leading from the front and want to be seen as the key policy-maker. John Major and James Callaghan (1976–79) were less dominant figures.
- **State of the economy.** The theory is that a healthy economy will usually help a prime minister, but John Major may have proved this theory wrong: the economy was in a bad way in 1992 and he won; it was in very good condition in 1997 and he lost.
- **Patronage.** Clever use of patronage (jobs) for rewarding loyalty will strengthen the prime minister's position. Margaret Thatcher was very good at exercising patronage; John Major was not.
- **Party divisions.** John Major was badly weakened by Conservative Party divisions over Europe; Tony Blair has been strengthened by the consistent appearance of unity in the Labour Party on all major matters.
- **Possible rivals.** The existence or non-existence of rivals to the prime minister's position will affect his or her exercise of power.
- **Electoral prospects.** The nearness of a general election and the governing party's current standing in the polls will affect prime ministerial power.

D Limits on a prime minister's power

A typical question might be on the key powers and limitations of a prime minister.

Although at times they are accused of being dictators, prime ministers have several important limits on their powers.

THE PARTY

On the whole, the prime minister's party inside and outside parliament will support the prime minister. However, there are cases when this has not happened:

- Conservative MPs rejected Margaret Thatcher and stopped her being prime minister in 1990.
- John Major was unable to pass legislation he wanted as several Conservative MPs voted against his measures in parliament.
- Tony Blair was unable to bring in the changes he wished to child benefit because of opposition within his party. He has also had to rethink his policy on fuel taxation and pensions because of pressure from his party.

PUBLIC OPINION

This is always an unpredictable force. It was public pressure that forced the Conservatives under Margaret Thatcher and John Major to abandon the poll tax. Public opinion has been a major factor in preventing radical reform of the health service since 1979: all prime ministers have wished to deal with the soaring costs of it, but have failed. Tony Blair is reluctant to move as far and as fast as he would like on the euro because of a hostile public opinion.

PARLIAMENT

Parliament, of course, has the power to remove a prime minister at any time. James Callaghan was removed by a vote of the House of Commons against him in 1979 and Margaret Thatcher came close to it over the Westland Affair in the 1980s. With limited control over the House of Lords and quite effective scrutiny powers in select committees, parliament can make life difficult for prime ministers, as John Major discovered over the Maastricht Treaty.

THE CABINET

A cabinet united against a policy of the prime minister can act as quite a strong brake. Perhaps this is one of the reasons why recent prime ministers have tended to meet the whole cabinet much less frequently.

Tony Blair (up to 2001) did not have real difficulties with his cabinet; they were loyal and supportive. However, Mrs Thatcher found her first cabinet (1979–83) difficult and she was forced to compromise over Rhodesia and public spending cuts. John Major found his cabinet after 1992 very difficult to manage, and it proved to be a major brake on his European policy.

Prime ministers have no department of their own, and if they want a policy implemented, it is the relevant minister who actually has to carry it out. If only one minister strongly opposes a plan, he or she can be sacked and replaced or forced to resign, as Margaret Thatcher did to Michael Heseltine over the Westland helicopter sale. However, if all the cabinet are strongly opposed, then it is difficult to sack them all. When Harold Macmillan sacked seven cabinet ministers in one day, his authority and government never really recovered.

E Prime ministerial styles

Note how much of the style and work of Callaghan was forced on him by his lack of a majority in parliament.

JAMES CALLAGHAN (LABOUR), 1976–79

Much of Callaghan's work as prime minister was dictated by the fact that he did not have a majority in the House of Commons, and was therefore dependent on another party, the Liberals, to stay in power. He also had to pay much more attention to the demands of his backbenchers than most prime ministers. He and his chancellor of the exchequer once lost a major part of their budget when two Labour backbenchers voted against it. To keep his party in parliament in order, he was forced to keep left-wingers in his cabinet, such as Tony Benn who opposed him and his more moderate ideas. In the end Callaghan got through the main policies he wished, but was also forced to accept policies, such as devolution for Scotland and Wales, which he disliked. He had to listen to and heed the wishes of his cabinet and his parliamentary party much more than other prime ministers have had to. He also suffered the indignity of being the last prime minister to be defeated in the House of Commons on a motion of no confidence. He was not a dominating figure because he did not have the opportunity to be so. A background of severe economic difficulties, with rising inflation and unemployment, did not help his situation either. He was also in his sixties when he took office, and had not been seen as a particularly successful minister when in government in the 1960s.

Remember that in spite of her power and achievements, Thatcher was prime minister one day and a backbench MP the next, as a result of her own parliamentary party turning against her.

MARGARET THATCHER (CONSERVATIVE), 1979–90

Margaret Thatcher was always seen as having a very different style from both Callaghan and her successor, John Major. The main features of her premiership were the consistency and firmness of her ideas. She also won three elections in a row and this gave her the conviction that the public endorsed her. She saw her role as to lead from the front, and she was quite determined to eliminate any opposition to her ideas, be they in her cabinet, her party, parliament or anywhere else. When she felt that the Greater London Council (led by Ken Livingstone) and the Metropolitan Councils were always going to oppose her views, she abolished them. She reduced the civil service by more than a third and privatised huge sections of British industry. She was a radical who imposed radical solutions to problems. She was immensely hard working and took great care to dominate all sections of government. She preferred not to wait until there was a **consensus** (broad agreement) for a policy within her government, but considered that ministers in the government were there to carry out her ideas.

Key aspects of Thatcher's style:
- abrasive
- dominating
- radical
- intolerant of opposition
- innovative

JOHN MAJOR (CONSERVATIVE), 1990–97

John Major had a very different personality from Margaret Thatcher, and preferred to listen more to cabinet and party. In addition he did not have an effective majority after the election of 1992. While Margaret Thatcher's status was boosted by the successful Falklands War in 1982, the public judged John Major by the economic disaster of the exchange rate mechanism in 1992. He seemed to be forced on to the defensive and was weakened by endless accusations of 'sleaze' in his party and defeats over Europe. He was further weakened by a sustained and bitter press campaign against him and his government. He certainly hoped to be less dominant than Margaret Thatcher, but did not wish to be as weak as he was.

Key aspects of Major's style:
- listened to party
- less dominant and dominating
- worked more with cabinet and sought consensus
- allowed ministers to dominate policy in their department, e.g. Kenneth Clarke at the Treasury
- indecisive

TONY BLAIR (LABOUR), 1997–PRESENT

Many commentators feel that Tony Blair is similar to Margaret Thatcher. He has strong views, is seen as a 'conviction' politician and demands more control over government, party and parliament than any Labour predecessor.

Key aspects of Blair's style:
- more direct control over government departments
- fewer and shorter cabinet meetings
- more decisions made by the prime minister working with individual cabinet members
- central control of government information and media management by Alastair Campbell
- less attention paid to parliament and the wishes of the parliamentary party
- great emphasis on his 'image'
- less use of civil servants and more use of his own policy advisers
- use of the Prime Minister's Office rather than the cabinet as the central co-ordinating body of the administration

It is vital to have a good knowledge of the work of Tony Blair from 1997 to the present — the Number 10 website will give lots of help here!

F Debates on prime ministerial power

Candidates should know something of the academic debates about the merits and demerits of prime ministerial power. Look up the Crossman thesis, which argued in the 1960s that the prime minister had replaced the cabinet as the major force in the British system of government. Note also Tony Benn's ideas on how the powers of the prime minister could be reduced, and also Quintin Hogg's ideas on the prime minister being an 'elected dictator'. At present the main debate is on whether the prime minister is becoming 'presidential' and taking on a role similar to that of the president of the United States.

The main reasons for seeing the prime minister as increasingly presidential are as follows:

- He has increasing control over appointments, especially in the civil service.
- He is dominating the policy-making process much more.
- He is appearing as the sole national leader, rather than the cabinet being seen as having power.
- He is being projected much more as a leader by the media.
- He is spending less time in the House of Commons and is accused of no longer viewing it as an important part of the political process.
- More key advisers are working for him, and not for the government as a whole.

With regard to this debate, it is useful to compare the position of the British prime minister with those of the American and French presidents.

It is ironic to note that most American presidents wish they had the same degree of power as the British prime minister.

THE AMERICAN PRESIDENT

Don't see the American president as an all-powerful official and Tony Blair and Margaret Thatcher as British prime ministers trying to become as 'presidential' or as powerful as, for example, President Bush. The American president is severely restricted by the written American constitution, which was designed to ensure that the American executive never became as powerful as the British system they had broken away from. The American president, although directly elected by the American people, is severely restricted in several ways.

- All the president's ministerial appointments have to be vetted by Congress (parliament) and Congress may have an opposition majority.
- The president does not have the ability to introduce and influence legislation in the same way as the British prime minister.
- Congress has much greater control over the budget and foreign policy than the British Parliament.
- There are broad areas of American life, such as education, crime and punishment, over which the president has virtually no influence at all.
- The president even has very limited control over the economy.

So despite having a huge nuclear arsenal, the American president simply does not have the ability to carry out policy and introduce legislation as freely as the British prime minister.

Compare Tony Blair with the French president if you are considering the debate on whether the British premiership is becoming 'presidential'.

THE FRENCH PRESIDENT

A much better example of 'presidential' power lies within the EU — in the office of the French president, which possesses much greater power. The French president:

- is elected directly, not by a political party or its MPs, as in the UK
- appoints the prime minister and assists the prime minister with other key appointments
- chairs the Council of Ministers
- has a veto over legislation
- takes key decisions on whether to call referendums
- can dissolve the French parliament
- makes key appointments outside the government, such as heads of the armed services

- is commander-in-chief of the armed services
- controls all key foreign and defence policy issues
- has considerable influence over the management of the economy
- does not have to attend occasions such as Question Time — and is generally seen as a much less accountable figure than the British prime minister

G Key terms and concepts

Authority The ability to get people to do things because they think that an individual, such as the prime minister, has the right to tell them what to do. It is a variable: a prime minister's authority over his or her parliamentary party may increase if the prime minister wins elections and his or her policies prove popular with the electors.

Power The ability to get things done, or make others do things that they may not want to do. The prime minister had the 'power' to move Robin Cook in 2001 from the Foreign Office to lead the House of Commons.

Knowledge of this topic is required by all three examination boards, but very much as a 'follow on' from the prime minister. There is nevertheless a strong possibility of a direct question on the cabinet, with a particular focus on its role.

Key questions

What is the role of the cabinet and how well does it perform it?

What is meant by the collective responsibility of the cabinet and how important is it to the British system of government?

Does the cabinet still have an important role to play in the British system of government?

A Development of the cabinet

The main role of the cabinet was developed in the eighteenth century.

EIGHTEENTH-CENTURY ORIGINS

Like the office of the prime minister, the cabinet developed into its present role during the eighteenth century. By 1800 it was established that the cabinet contained the prime minister and the key ministers, and that it was in the cabinet that major policy decisions were made. All members of the cabinet sat in either the House of Lords or the House of Commons, and they dominated the legislative process in parliament. It was accepted that members of the cabinet should agree on policy, support each other's ideas and resign together if the government was defeated in parliament.

As with the office of the prime minister, the cabinet has undergone only minor changes in its role since the early nineteenth century.

CHANGES IN THE NINETEENTH AND TWENTIETH CENTURIES

The cabinet has tended to grow in size. The main reason for this is that the role of government has expanded and the areas where the government intervenes, such as agriculture and health, have necessitated having key ministers in the central decision-making body.

In wartime, such as 1914–18, the cabinet set up key small subcommittees to run the war, as a body of 20+ people was not ideal for rapid decision making. The cabinet also gained a very efficient secretariat in 1916 to ensure that proper records were kept of decisions, and that decisions were communicated to the relevant departments.

B Aspects of the modern cabinet

The size of the cabinet is a major reason why it is no longer the dominant part of the executive.

CABINET SIZE

Modern prime ministers have found it difficult to keep the cabinet below 22 members. Attempts have been made to reduce it in size but, for example, farmers might get offended if they were not represented in the cabinet, as no doubt would the Scots, Northern Irish and Welsh. There has been much talk among academics of reducing the cabinet in size and having 'superministers' who might look after several areas, such as defence, foreign policy and international development, or education and culture. However, it is unlikely that there will be any change in the cabinet's overall size. As well as making sure all interests feel represented, the prime minister also needs a large number of 'top' jobs to reward loyal and able colleagues, and ensure that all sections of the party are represented at cabinet level.

CABINET MEMBERSHIP

The key members of the cabinet and their individual roles have to be known.

By convention (unwritten rule), all members of the cabinet have to be members of the House of Commons or the House of Lords. Most have specific roles, such as the chancellor of the exchequer or the secretary of state for social security. Some may just have a party function, such as the chief whip or the leader of the House of Commons, who has the task of getting the government's programme of legislation through parliament.

Cabinet members also all have to be privy councillors (an office created in the sixteenth century) and as a result have to take an important oath of secrecy about all government business. They are all governed by a very strict code of conduct, and breach of this, as in the cases of Peter Mandelson and David Mellor, leads to the prime minister requiring their resignations.

COLLECTIVE RESPONSIBILITY

This convention applies to all members of the government, but is particularly important for members of the cabinet. It states that once a decision has been made by the cabinet — for example, to implement a tax increase — then all members of the cabinet have to support it fully, even if they argued against it in cabinet. If they cannot accept the responsibility for the decision and back it fully in parliament and outside, then they must resign.

This 'rule' gives the appearance of unity to a government, and it is important for members of the cabinet who have to take unpopular decisions, such as a tax increase, to know that they will be supported by all the other members of the government. Margaret Thatcher insisted on collective responsibility, and at least two very senior cabinet ministers, Michael Heseltine and Geoffrey Howe, resigned because they could not support her government's policy.

John Major tolerated much more public disagreement among cabinet ministers, especially over Europe with ministers like Michael Portillo and John Redwood, but the appearance of real disunity over such a major issue may have been an important factor in the Conservative defeat in the election of 1997.

Collective responsibility is still an important and well-maintained convention under Tony Blair.

Tony Blair has insisted on collective responsibility very strongly and successfully, and his cabinet of 1997–2001 was visibly united and always 'sang from the same hymn sheet'. This may have been an important factor in his success in winning the 2001 general election. The voting public likes to see unity in its government (and shadow cabinet).

A more recent example of a minister resigning over the issue of collective responsibility was in 1999 when Peter Kilfoyle, who was not in the cabinet but a junior minister, resigned from the Labour government as he felt that it was not spending enough time and effort on its core voters.

Critics of collective responsibility argue that it is wrong for ministers to have to defend policies that they (a) are known to have disagreed with and (b) had no part in drafting.

THE CURRENT ROLE OF THE CABINET

At present the cabinet has several key roles:

- It acts as the central clearing house for key decisions, although these may have been taken elsewhere.
- It plays a vital part in the co-ordination of all government activities — the heads of every major department and function in the UK (such as policing) are there.
- It is where major policies get endorsed by all members of the government.
- Any crisis — be it war or a fuel shortage — will be managed by some of its members.
- It might put a brake on a prime minister or a radical minister.
- It sets the agenda for parliament.
- It referees disputes between departments.
- It provides the vital link between party, parliament, the legal system and the government — it joins all parts of our system of government together.

If key decisions are no longer taken much in cabinet meetings, as it is a large group and only meets for a short time each week, then one member of the cabinet or a small group of cabinet members will take them.

Under prime ministers such as Harold Wilson (1964–70, 1974–76) and James Callaghan (1976–79), the cabinet was very much the decision-making body in the UK. However, under Margaret Thatcher its role as a decision-maker declined significantly and the role of the cabinet changed fundamentally. The key decisions were made by the prime minister in consultation with individual ministers and advisers. This process has continued under Tony Blair, who, it is argued, has adopted not only many of Margaret Thatcher's policies, but also her style of managing the cabinet.

CABINET COMMITTEES

Increasingly large amounts of business that were once done in the full cabinet are now being delegated to cabinet committees. These are small groups of cabinet members, appointed by the prime minister, who deal with specific issues. There are two types:

- **Standing committees of the cabinet.** An example is the Economic Affairs Committee, which will of course have the chancellor of the exchequer on it, together with other members chosen by the prime minister. Their main role is the planning of British economic policy. This committee will also have a key influence on public spending.
- **Ad hoc committees.** These are set up for a specific purpose and closed down when their work is finished. Margaret Thatcher set one up to deal with the miners' strike of 1984–85, and Tony Blair set one up to plan reforms to the House of Lords.

Cabinet committees have a small membership and so are more efficient than the full cabinet. They also have more time to consult experts. It is usual for their decisions and recommendations to be accepted by the rest of the cabinet. Only in serious disputes in committee, such as over the Westland affair under Mrs Thatcher, will the matter go to the full cabinet for a decision.

There is some evidence to suggest that Tony Blair is making less use of both the full cabinet and cabinet committees, and prefers to make decisions and policy in discussion with individual ministers and policy advisers.

CHANGES TO THE CABINET COMMITTEE SYSTEM IN 2001

After the general election victory of 2001, Tony Blair decided to make major changes in the system of cabinet committees. At the time of writing (August 2001) there are 44 cabinet committees — a small increase on 1997–2001.

The biggest change is that one new over-arching cabinet committee on domestic affairs has been set up, chaired by the deputy prime minister, John Prescott. The objective of this committee is to oversee policy innovations and to bring more coherence to the government. In the past, the cabinet as a whole would normally have performed this function.

This committee will be underpinned by nine subcommittees, which have specific responsibility for areas such as drugs policy, rural renewal and social exclusion. The prime minister, of course, decides membership of these committees, and it is possible for junior ministers to be involved in them.

Some commentators argue that this new 'over-arching committee' is designed to reduce the influence of the chancellor Gordon Brown and his department, the Treasury, over the government and its policy-making processes. However, the chancellor will have a seat on this new committee and he will also chair the vital cabinet committee that decides public spending.

John Prescott will also chair a new cabinet committee on the nations and regions, designed to enhance their place in New Labour thinking. Robin Cook, the leader of the House of Commons, is chairing key committees on constitutional reform and on the legislative programme for parliament.

It is also seen as significant that Charles Clarke, the new Labour Party chairman, has been given a seat on key cabinet committees, such as:

- Economic Affairs
- Future Legislation
- Domestic Affairs
- Public Spending
- Constitutional Reform
- European Policy

The reason for this is felt to be that Tony Blair wants the views of the party and its activists represented in the key areas of decision making.

The Cabinet Office, which services the cabinet and its committees, has been expanded and strengthened, and a 'Progress-Chasing Unit' has been added to it to ensure that policy decisions that are made by the cabinet are followed through and put into practice.

This is a simple and straightforward topic that requires study for all three of the examination boards. The focus needs to be on the role of ministers and their accountability.

Key questions

What is meant by ministerial responsibility?

What is the importance of the convention of ministerial responsibility?

When and why do ministers resign?

What is the role of ministers?

Who has power within the executive?

How accountable is the executive?

A Different types of government minister

CABINET MINISTERS

Cabinet ministers are the heads of the major departments of state. A good example of the responsibilities of a cabinet minister is the foreign secretary, who will be expected to:

- take responsibility for the conduct of foreign policy
- do further cabinet work, sit on key cabinet committees and share responsibility for the whole conduct of government policy
- answer questions in parliament and appear before select committees of the House of Commons to deal with issues arising out of his or her department's work
- ensure that any legislation covering foreign affairs passes through parliament
- travel widely and visit other countries
- be involved in political party work, as a senior member of a political party
- spend time dealing with constituency matters, as an elected MP
- attend and vote in the House of Commons on key bills

There is some debate as to whether cabinet ministers have too many roles and are not able to perform them all properly. However, cabinet ministers do receive a substantial additional salary over and above what they get as MPs.

MINISTERS OF STATE

There are usually about 29 of these. One or two of them will be allocated to major departments such as the Foreign Office. They will be given specific areas of responsibility under the cabinet minister: for example, Tony Blair has appointed a 'minister for Europe', who has a particular responsibility for the relationship between the UK and the EU. The minister for Europe will report both to the foreign secretary and to the prime minister. Ministers of state get an additional salary and may well be expected to answer questions in parliament and help get legislation through. About 20% may progress into the cabinet, but for the majority this is as high up the promotion ladder as they will go.

PARLIAMENTARY UNDERSECRETARIES

This is the lowest rung of the ministerial ladder. Like ministers of state and cabinet ministers, parliamentary undersecretaries will be paid an additional salary and be assigned specific responsibilities within a department. They are expected to do a lot of public relations work for a department in parliament, help legislation through and also deal with the late-night adjournment debates in the Commons. There are about 36 of them in all. This post is seen very much as a 'testing' ground for future cabinet ministers, as success at this level will lead to promotion.

The total number of ministers — those paid salaries in addition to their pay as an MP — is about 100.

B The role of ministers

Ministers of state and parliamentary undersecretaries (all known as junior ministers) do as they are told, so we will focus on the work of the cabinet minister. The cabinet minister's key roles are:

- to provide policy in the minister's area of responsibility, e.g. home affairs in the case of the home secretary
- to provide legislation in his or her area, e.g. a new Education Bill
- to deal with emergencies affecting his or her area, e.g. the foot-and-mouth crisis of 2001
- to manage the department and take responsibility for its work, e.g. the foreign secretary dealt with press questions about the way in which demonstrators at the G8 conference in Genoa (2001) had been treated
- to take full responsibility for everything that happens in his or her 'area' — and for what should have happened but didn't, e.g. when questions were raised in parliament and in the press about the performance of military equipment in the Kosovo conflict, the defence secretary had to deal with them, accept responsibility for the failings and take steps to ensure they were not repeated
- to share responsibility for all government policy with cabinet colleagues, and this means decisions that a minister may have had no part in taking at all
- to be accountable to parliament, giving oral and written answers, attending relevant standing and select committees, adjournment debates and opposition days
- to market, defend and promote his or her department and its policies, particularly through the media — being able to manage the media is a vital skill
- to be a good constituency MP, really representing and looking after individual constituents
- to be a good MP generally, listening to backbenchers and attending parliament regularly
- to be a good member of his or her party, which may mean making speeches, participating in television programmes such as *Question Time* and helping in by-elections

There is a strong case for arguing that ministers are overloaded and cannot perform effectively.

You might consider this workload and responsibilities. Is it reasonable to ask so much of one individual? Can the UK be well served by people who have so much to do? Perhaps the Americans have the right idea when they forbid anyone from being both a minister and a member of their parliament (Congress). This is known as the **separation of powers** and means that a person is not allowed to be a member of the legislature and a member of the executive.

C Ministerial responsibility

Ministerial responsibility is a vital part of the whole democratic process, as it is through this process that citizens and taxpayers can call those who take decisions on their behalf to account. It means that a minister is accountable for all that happens in his or her area of responsibility.

For example, the secretary of state for defence is responsible for all matters concerning the defence of the UK. If the RAF proves to be incompetent in a war, then it is the minister's responsibility to take the blame for this, find out what happened, discipline those who have failed and take steps to ensure that it does not happen again. The minister will have to explain this to parliament and the media, and to cabinet colleagues and the prime minister.

If there is clear evidence that the minister has been incompetent or made a major error of judgement, then he or she must resign. Lord Carrington, foreign secretary in 1982, resigned over his failure to foresee the Argentinian invasion of the Falklands.

AREAS OF MINISTERIAL RESPONSIBILITY

There are two main areas of ministerial responsibility:

Ensure that you know three or four recent examples of ministers resigning when they made major errors of judgement over policy.

- **Role responsibility.** This is the responsibility ministers have for their department, for getting necessary laws through, for making necessary policy and for the general management of their department. When a major error of judgement or serious mismanagement occurs, resignation is expected. For example, in 1992 the economy suffered a major reverse over the exchange rate mechanism and interest rates soared. The chancellor, Norman Lamont, eventually resigned. Both the foreign secretary, Lord Carrington, and the minister of state at the foreign office, Richard Luce, resigned in 1982 when the UK was surprised by the Argentinian invasion of the Falklands.
- **Personal responsibility.** This means that ministers have to take responsibility for their own personal conduct. If they either break the law or indulge in behaviour that the public, the media and the prime minister do not approve of, then they have to resign. There are many recent examples of this. In 1998 the secretary of state for Wales resigned over what he called a 'moment of madness' on Clapham Common. In the same year the secretary of state for trade and industry, Peter Mandelson, was forced to resign when it was revealed that he had 'forgotten' to declare that he had been lent a large sum of money by Geoffrey Robinson, another minister, whose business dealings Mandelson's department was investigating. Peter Mandelson was brought back into the

cabinet as secretary of state for Northern Ireland, but had to resign again when questions were raised in the media about the assistance he may have given to Indian citizens who desired British passports, and who had also donated money to the Millennium Dome.

There are an increasing number of examples where the convention does not seem to have worked in practice.

FLAWS IN MINISTERIAL RESPONSIBILITY

The main failing with the principle is that it does not always seem to work. In the case of the BSE disaster, blame could not be allotted until long after the relevant ministers had left office, and the civil servants had retired or moved to other responsibilities.

If the minister retains the support of the prime minister, as in the case of William Waldegrave over the sale of arms to Iraq in 1989–90, nothing happens. In the case of alleged salmonella in eggs, it was the junior minister Edwina Currie (not the cabinet minister) who was forced to resign, after a sustained campaign by Tory backbenchers and the National Farmers' Union demanding a scapegoat.

The **convention** (an unwritten rule that has the force of a law) is fine in theory. The public ought to know who must shoulder the responsibility for mistakes. However, it seems to vary in practice. An important example is the case of the former home secretary Michael Howard. In 1995, there were some serious escapes by major criminals from British prisons. Prisons are the responsibility of the home secretary, but Howard did not resign. Instead he sacked the head of the Prison Agency, maintaining that it was his fault. But in 1998, long after Michael Howard had left office, it was discovered that 'Howard had failed to provide parliament with information, which if known at the time, might have resulted in his being forced to resign.' With more and more decisions being taken by unelected quangos and heads of agencies (see Unit 6), responsibility can be difficult to allocate.

The Scott Report of 1996 condemned several ministers for their conduct in the sale of arms to Iraq. This had been done in secret and in clear breach of official policy, which had been approved by parliament. In the end the prime minister, John Major, did not require any of them to resign, and in fact some of the relevant ministers and civil servants were promoted.

There is a growing feeling that the convention of ministerial responsibility lacks real 'teeth'. But if the media put on enough pressure, or raise sufficient public indignation over an issue, then the prime minister will stop trying to 'ride it out' and require resignation. When a prime minister asks a minister to resign, it is convention always to obey.

D Ministerial turnover

It has become increasingly common for ministers to be moved from department to department on a regular basis, or simply removed from office. In the major reshuffle of 1998, 52 ministers were moved and 13 were sacked. The main reasons for ministerial turnover are as follows:

- They have proved to be incompetent — perhaps good in opposition but not up to managing a department. Tony Blair may well have moved Jack Cunningham for this reason.
- There have been disagreements over policy. Frank Field was removed from his office in the Department of Social Security in 1998 for this reason.
- To stop the danger of ministers 'going native': in other words, being too strongly influenced by the (possibly conservative) ideas of the civil servants they are supposed to be leading.
- The prime minister wants to reward those who have been loyal and to demote those who have not. In recent years, Mo Mowlam may have come into the second category, and Alastair Darling and Stephen Byers into the first.

However, at the time of writing there is rather more stability and less ministerial turnover under Tony Blair than was the case under Margaret Thatcher. Blair had only one lord chancellor, one chancellor of the exchequer, one foreign secretary, one education secretary and one home secretary in the whole of his government from 1997 to 2001. The reshuffle that followed the general election of 2001 was quite extensive, but in many cases — such as the move of Robin Cook from the Foreign Office to being leader of the House of Commons — the changes were from one cabinet post to another. Few people actually left the cabinet for good.

The civil service is a specified topic with all three examination boards. A reasonable knowledge of the structure of the executive at this level is needed, but the main areas to focus on are accountability and the relationship between ministers and civil servants. Ensure you have a working knowledge of the ways in which agencies and quangos differ from 'normal' government departments, and the effect they have on accountability and ministerial responsibility.

Key questions

What is the role of the civil service?

Is the civil service too powerful?

How can the civil service be held accountable?

In what ways has the civil service been changed in recent years?

In what ways and to what extent have agencies and quangos changed the structure of the executive in the UK?

A Development of the civil service

ORIGINS OF THE CIVIL SERVICE

All monarchs needed help to administer the nation and collect taxes, so Britain always had a group of officials who served the state. By the middle of the nineteenth century it was becoming very clear that those who helped ministers to run the day-to-day business of their departments were simply not up to the job. When Britain went to war with Russia in the Crimea (1854–56), many thousands of soldiers died because of the incompetence of the support and supply services: in other words, the civil servants who helped administer the army and navy. A sustained press campaign, which pointed out their incompetence, led to major changes.

A disastrous war, caused partly by the civil service of the day, led to the first major reforms.

CHANGES IN THE MID-NINETEENTH CENTURY

Two men, Northcote and Trevelyan, led the inquiry into the civil service following the Crimean War. It recommended that in future civil servants be appointed not because they happened to be related to an important political figure, but on grounds of merit alone. The inquiry's main recommendations were as follows:

- Civil servants should be promoted on merit.
- Civil servants should be recruited through a tough competitive exam.
- The examination should be in the liberal arts.
- Men with technical expertise or experience in other walks of life were not welcome.

The aim was to obtain a small highly educated **elite** to advise ministers on policy. Although these men may not have been experts in economics or defence, it was assumed that they were intelligent enough to acquire the necessary expertise.

Gladstone laid down the broad outline of the modern civil service in the 1860s.

William Gladstone, who was firstly chancellor of the exchequer and then prime minister, put these ideas into practice. He also set up the Public Accounts Committee of the House of Commons to make sure that the money handed over by parliament to the civil service to spend on areas such as education was properly and honestly spent. Gladstone did much to make the civil service into an intellectually able group of great honesty and integrity. But there is some doubt about whether these men were the best equipped to give ministers policy advice in complex matters, given that most were educated in Latin and Greek.

The idea of an elite civil service was not a new one; it had been implemented over a thousand years earlier in China. The reason why top civil servants in this country are sometimes referred to as 'mandarins' is because that was the name of the top civil servants who served the Chinese emperor.

TWENTIETH-CENTURY DEVELOPMENTS IN THE CIVIL SERVICE

The intention of Gladstone, Northcote and Trevelyan was that an elected minister, chosen by the people and accountable to parliament, should be advised by a small elite group of civil servants on matters of policy. Once a policy had been decided by a minister after discussion with senior civil servants (e.g. to change the system of taxation) and parliament had approved it, then it would be handed over to more junior civil servants to carry out. The minister and parliament would ensure that the civil servants did the job properly.

As the role of government grew, so did the size and workload of the civil service.

However, the civil service grew rapidly in size, from a few thousand to over 750,000 men and women in the course of the twentieth century. The main reason for this was that the state took on more and more tasks which had to be administered, ranging from housing and education, to roads and health. Huge numbers of civil servants were needed to manage all these tasks.

CONCERNS IN THE LATE TWENTIETH CENTURY

From the middle of the twentieth century onwards, there were growing concerns about the civil service. They were as follows:

- It was not giving good advice to ministers. Civil servants were felt to be conservative and out of touch with contemporary needs.
- It had taken on tasks — such as running the telephone system — which it was unfit to do. There was a real lack of managerial expertise in the civil service.
- It had become far too big and expensive. Simply paying and providing office space for three-quarters of a million men and women was a huge drain on public spending.
- It was recruiting the wrong sort of individual. Selecting arts graduates from Oxford and Cambridge was not providing ministers with the informed and expert advice they needed.
- It was spending its time administering departments and not advising ministers on what might be the best policy options. Its role had changed from what had been intended.
- It was making too many mistakes — look up the Crichel Down affair and the spy scandal over Burgess and Maclean.
- It was not properly accountable — it was too vast for ministers to control and the public could not find out information about it.

- It was preventing the radical reform needed to deal with the UK's economy and social problems.
- The civil service was reluctant to retrain to adapt to new tasks; it was hostile to new ideas about how to carry out its tasks.
- It lacked technical skills and was hostile to experts.
- It lacked the management skills needed to run major departments that had thousands of employees.

THE WORK OF HAROLD WILSON, 1964–70

Harold Wilson, Labour prime minister between 1964 and 1970, had been a civil servant himself in the Second World War. When he came into power he was determined to reform the civil service. However, he was prevented from achieving much by the superb delaying tactics for which the civil service had become renowned. The TV series *Yes, Minister* and *Yes, Prime Minister*, in which civil servants stop elected ministers from doing what they are supposed to do, are based on real events.

Harold Wilson's two main aims were to make the civil service both more accountable and more professional. To increase accountability he set up the **ombudsman** (parliamentary commissioner for administration). The aims behind the creation of the ombudsman were:

- to enable citizens to complain to an independent body if they had a grievance about a civil servant (e.g. if they felt they had been made to pay too much tax — civil servants collect and assess tax)
- for that independent body to have the power to get all the details on the case
- to compensate citizens if they had been hard done by the civil servants
- to take steps to ensure that the civil servants involved did not repeat the harm they had done

Harold Wilson's attempted reforms failed totally.

In the end, however, none of these four aims was fulfilled. The ombudsman has limited power to investigate issues. There are several departments, such as defence and health, over which the ombudsman has virtually no powers at all. He or she has no disciplinary powers, and can only report 'maladministration'. The public has no direct access to the ombudsman; citizens have to go through their MP.

Wilson also tried to organise a full-scale study of the civil service — its role, its size, its functions, the quality of its advice, etc. This was ably blocked by the civil service, and the only result was the Fulton Report in 1968.

THE FULTON REPORT

This recommended:

- changes in training of civil servants, particularly junior ones. It was felt that senior civil servants did not need it
- changes in long-term planning by the civil service. It was suggested that each department, such as health, set up a section to deal with long-term planning. No machinery was instituted to ensure that this happened; nor was it considered what relationship this section might have to the rest of the department
- some changes in recruitment, again mainly at the lower levels. There was no suggestion that more expertise might be brought into the civil service

- the creation of a Civil Service Department, to 'manage' the civil service. The role of this new department (which, of course, involved hiring more civil servants to run it) was not thought through, and there is no evidence that it achieved much. Margaret Thatcher ultimately abolished it

Further attempts to reform the civil service in the 1970s failed.

Most of the reforms never really happened, and the few reforms that came in were later seen to fail. Both the Conservative governments of 1970–74 and the Labour government of 1974–79 were very dissatisfied with the support they gained from their civil servants.

Margaret Thatcher was very unhappy about the support she had received from her civil servants when she was a minister between 1970 and 1974. When she came to power in 1979 she was determined to change the civil service — and she did.

It could be argued that one of Margaret Thatcher's most radical policies was to reform the civil service.

THE THATCHER REFORMS

Margaret Thatcher (prime minister 1979–90) introduced a series of reforms that changed the civil service as radically as Gladstone's had a century before. Although she was opposed by the Labour opposition at the time, Tony Blair and his government have shown no sign of reversing her reforms. These were the key ones:

- The civil service was reduced in size from about 750,000 in 1979 to fewer than 500,000 when Thatcher left office.
- The Civil Service Department, which the prime minister felt was too 'soft' on civil service pay and conditions, was abolished. Control over the civil service was given to the Treasury, which took a much more hard-line view on pay, promotion and conditions of service.
- Performance-related pay was introduced and the government started to reduce the job security that civil servants had enjoyed.
- An Efficiency Unit was set up under an outside businessman, Derek Rayner, to reduce costs. It led to millions of pounds of savings, but not quite the billions Thatcher had hoped for.
- The Financial Management Initiative was instituted. The aim was to bring much more efficient management practices, such as clear target setting, into the civil service. It was hoped to encourage initiative, end bureaucracy and introduce more expertise.
- Privatisation and market testing were introduced. Some functions that had always been performed by the civil service, such as developing software for civil service computers, were contracted out to private companies. There had been a Department for Energy, but as gas and electricity were sold off, these departments were no longer needed. Market testing required civil servants to compete with outsiders for their jobs.
- Margaret Thatcher took care to interview candidates for the top posts in the civil service. In the past, ministers had tended to accept the advice of their civil servants. Thatcher insisted on interviewing them personally, and frequently rejected her civil servants' advice. She was looking for more radical men and women who were prepared to show commitment to her aims and objectives. This led to the famous quote 'Is he one of us?' — in other words, did the person in question support her radical agenda?

These reforms all had some effect, but by 1987 it was felt that the civil service still required further reform. As a result, Thatcher asked a prominent businessman, Robin Ibbs, to report on the civil service.

THE IBBS REPORT — THE 'NEXT STEPS' PROGRAMME

When Ibbs examined the civil service, he found that it was too big, it lacked innovative talent, it failed to provide the taxpayer with value for money, it placed too little focus on quality advice for ministers, and it spent too much time administering things inefficiently. He made the following recommendations:

- The administrative functions of the civil service, such as dealing with driving licences and collecting taxes, should be handed over to agencies. These should be separate from ordinary civil service/government departments such as the Foreign Office. These new agencies would specialise in one particular area, such as prisons or immigration.
- 95% of civil servants should work in agencies, taking their broad instructions from ministers (e.g. toughening up the driving test) and then using their own managerial skills to administer that policy properly.
- Only a few of the 'traditional' civil servants should remain in London and other cities, advising ministers on policy. They would form about 5% of the total and focus on policy advice. It was hoped that they would be more innovative and radical than their predecessors, and not weighed down by administering vast departments.

Mrs Thatcher left office in 1990, before being able to carry out these ideas, but John Major (1990–97) did.

CIVIL SERVICE REFORMS UNDER JOHN MAJOR, 1990–97

By 1998 124 agencies had been set up, such as the Prison Agency which runs prisons under the broad instructions of the home secretary. These agencies employed nearly 75% of all civil servants. Some are huge, such as the Benefits Agency which employs over 70,000 people; others have only a few hundred, such as the Royal Mint. Tony Blair's government has continued the programme. This includes further privatisation, such as that of Department of Social Security property.

Although ridiculed at the time, partly for its famous 'cones hotline', John Major's idea for a Citizen's Charter was sound and it has become firmly established. The aim was to ensure that citizens received better service from civil servants, particularly those agencies and departments that came into contact with the public, such as the passport office and employment centres.

Each agency had to publish performance targets. The results they achieved were to be published, and also there had to be a clear and known way for the public to complain about poor service and receive compensation. There was to be a real focus in departments and agencies on serving the public well. It was hoped that they would be both 'civil' to and good 'servants' of the public.

SERVICE FIRST

This is largely the same as the Citizen's Charter, but is the name given to it by the Blair government of 1997–2001, possibly because it had been so critical of the Citizen's Charter when in opposition. A small team in the Cabinet Office runs

Tony Blair and John Major continued with Margaret Thatcher's radical changes.

The objectives of the Citizen's Charter need to be known.

Tony Blair has continued the process of checking the civil service and reducing its role.

it, and they put a lot of pressure on departments and agencies to respond quickly to public queries and concerns.

B Aspects of the modern civil service

A question on the nature and extent of civil service accountability is very possible.

MONITORING OF THE CIVIL SERVICE

The main ways in which the civil service is monitored and taxpayers can ensure they get value for money are as follows:

- The minister is always in charge and has the final say over appointments, conduct and policy. The minister is almost invariably an elected MP (although a few might be members of the House of Lords) and therefore 'represents' the democratic process.
- People have rights of complaint and redress under the Citizen's Charter.
- They can complain to the ombudsman (the parliamentary commissioner for administration), who can investigate some complaints and publicise incompetence by the civil service.
- Select committees of the House of Commons have the ability to question civil servants.
- When civil servants break the law — for example, by taking bribes — they can, of course, be prosecuted.
- MPs can question ministers in parliament about civil servants.
- The Public Accounts Committee of the House of Commons can monitor all that a department spends.
- The media can highlight incompetence or failure.

THE ROLE OF THE HIGHER CIVIL SERVANT

The primary role of senior civil servants is to advise ministers. It is their job to give ministers the information they want and need, and to advise them impartially to the best of their ability and using their experience. They should warn ministers of the consequences of their actions. Once the minister has made a decision, however, it is the job of civil servants to carry out that task to the very best of their abilities, whether they agree with it or not. Civil servants should remain anonymous, impartial and neutral when carrying out their duties. They must not divulge any information about their work unless ordered to do so by their minister.

Clearly there can be major difficulties in the relationship between ministers and their civil servants. Democracy requires that the civil servant carry out the wishes of the democratically elected minister. However, if the minister, who might be both ignorant and wrong, insists on a policy that an able and experienced civil servant knows will harm citizens, then what should the civil servant do?

THE IMPACT OF THE CONSERVATIVE REFORMS

The civil service is now smaller and cheaper, and certainly more efficient, than before 1979. The general feeling among Labour ministers is that they are getting better advice and service than their predecessors did in 1974–79. There have been no complaints about conservative groups of civil servants hindering Labour's radical programme. However, it is worth noting that the Labour government of 1997–2001 employed exactly double the number of 'political advisers' that John Major did, so Labour ministers are taking their advice more from those outside Whitehall.

On the other hand, there have been concerns that the civil service is too 'politicised' — that it worries too much about appealing to its current political masters and not about giving ministers the best advice, or protecting the public from the incompetence of ministers. There is also concern that it is difficult for ministers, and thus the public, to control the new agencies, and that democracy has suffered as a result.

The changing role of the civil service is another very likely question.

C The non-civil service

THE GROWTH OF POLITICAL ADVISERS

Ministers are increasingly taking advice on policy from non-civil servants.

An important development under Margaret Thatcher, which has been continued by Tony Blair, is the appointment of political advisers. In the past, ministers took their advice almost entirely from established and experienced civil servants. Now all senior ministers have the ability to appoint political advisers. These advisers can come from many different backgrounds and are given a salary similar to a senior civil servant. Their job is to offer advice to the minister on topics of the minister's choice. They have access to all the information a department has. They can be resented by the established and experienced civil servants.

QUANGOS

'Quango' stands for quasi-autonomous non-governmental organisation. Quangos are groups of people who are not civil servants or local government officers, who are given responsibility for a particular public task. The members of a quango are appointed by the relevant minister, are accountable to that minister, are paid and may be either full or part time.

Typical functions performed by quangos are:
- recommending to the secretary of state for education how much money should go to each university. The quango would also lay down the criteria by which universities get public money. Another quango inspects universities and publishes the university 'league tables'
- monitoring the examination boards. The secretary of state for education asked the head of QCA (the quango that monitors all public exams) for a report in the summer of 2001 on the new AS exams and how to improve them. The secretary of state did not ask the inspectors from her own department
- monitoring new drugs before they are used on the public
- running hospitals
- regulating the recently privatised industries, such as electricity

The role of quangos can be:
- executive, in that they have the power to act (e.g. to run prisons)

- advisory, in that they can recommend actions to the minister (e.g. to reduce the number of exams at AS)
- regulatory, in that they can agree, or forbid, activities in certain industries (e.g. regulating price rises in privatised industries such as telecommunications)

Expect the standard merits/demerits type of question here.

DISADVANTAGES OF QUANGOS

There are several criticisms of quangos:

- Their members are not elected and are only accountable to a minister.
- They control huge amounts of public money (probably about 40% of public spending now).
- Ministers make appointments, and ministers are accused of giving well-paid jobs to their friends and supporters.
- It can be difficult for the public to find out information about them.
- There is no real link between the tax-paying public and the quangos, which spend a lot of their money. It is argued that this is not right in a democracy.

ADVANTAGES OF QUANGOS

The number of quangos has grown steadily over the past 20 years. Their main merits are seen to be as follows:

- Experts can be used on a quango.
- Controversial issues, such as race relations and the content of school curricula, can be dealt with by impartial and independent experts, and removed from politics.
- Quangos tend to be quicker and cheaper than using civil servants and local government officials.
- Ministers can put their own supporters on a quango and rely on them to carry out the government's wishes. In contrast, civil servants or local authorities might slow down or obstruct government wishes.
- In enabling an elected government to achieve its objectives and manifesto promises, it could be argued that quangos are an aid to democracy.

This is a major topic for all three examination boards. The main areas to focus on are evident from the list of key questions below. A good working knowledge of the functioning of parliament is needed, and also the ability to comment on how well those functions are performed. You are strongly recommended to use the House of Commons website and to look at recent examples of parliamentary procedures, such as Question Time, adjournment debates and the workings of select and standing committees.

Key questions

What is the role and significance of parliament?

How well does parliament fulfil its role?

How does parliament scrutinise the executive?

What is the role of party in parliament?

How effective is the opposition in parliament?

What is the role of the backbench MP?

Is there a need to reform parliament?

A The development of parliament

The modern British Parliament is the product of a very long tradition.

PARLIAMENT TO 1600

There is evidence of a type of parliament, where the monarch consulted with his principal subjects on matters of great national importance, before the Norman Conquest of 1066. By 1500 the monarch was meeting regularly with two separate Houses of Parliament and gaining their consent for major issues such as taxation. The 'Upper' House was made up of the hereditary peerage and the senior clergy, while the 'lower' House of Commons was made up of elected men, usually two from each major town or city and two from each county.

It is worth noting that the Tudor monarchs ensured that all the major laws changing the religions of England were passed through parliament. By the end of the sixteenth century it was well established and accepted by all that a law which the king put forward, and which was supported by both Houses of Parliament, was superior to all other forms of law, and had to be obeyed even by the monarch.

PARLIAMENT FROM 1600 TO THE PRESENT

Two main features stand out in the development of parliament in this period:
- the gradual supremacy that parliament gained over the monarch
- the supremacy that the executive gained over parliament

By 1850 the monarch had to sign bills that she or he did not like, had to create peers to get bills through the House of Lords and had to accept the prime minister and cabinet that parliament and the electorate had chosen.

The growing dominance of parliament by the executive is a major feature of twentieth-century constitutional development.

The twentieth century has seen the government of the day, provided it has a majority in the House of Commons, controlling most of what parliament debates and legislates.

B Functions of the House of Commons

- **Legislation.** A key function of the Commons is to make laws, which are binding on everyone in the UK. This might be a law that imposes speed limits on cars, or devolves power to a Scottish Parliament.
- **Executive scrutiny.** The Commons has been entrusted with the key role of checking the actions of the government and all state employees, such as civil servants, and ensuring the vital principle of accountability. MPs have the power to dismiss governments or ministers, and to make them explain their actions.
- **Representation.** Each MP comes from a specific part of the country, called a **constituency** (usually made up of about 75,000 voters). MPs must look after the interests of the individuals in that constituency, and the area in general, and speak up in parliament on their behalf. MPs also represent the party of which they are a member, and may also represent other groups, such as trade unions or farmers, who give them financial backing.
- **Debate.** We expect the House of Commons to debate the great issues of the day, be it foreign policy towards Serbia or the future of genetic engineering. We expect the government of the day to listen to the ideas put forward by our representatives, and to have our own understanding of these issues enhanced by this public debate.
- **To provide ministers.** Almost all British ministers, including the prime minister, come from the House of Commons. Unlike in the USA, where there is a separation of powers and you cannot be a member of both the legislature and the executive, in the UK all ministers have to be members of parliament. Whether it is right for the House of Commons both to provide ministers and then to try to check them is an important issue.

A standard question is one that focuses on the functions of the House of Commons and how well they are performed.

C Members of Parliament

How 'representative' are MPs? Table 7.1 shows the main background of MPs elected in the 1997 general election. An outline knowledge of these statistics is needed to deal with questions about how representative parliament is.

THE ROLE OF BACKBENCHERS IN THE HOUSE OF COMMONS

Most MPs are backbenchers. The simplest definition of a backbench MP is one who is not allowed to sit on the two front benches, directly in front of the speaker in the House of Commons. Backbenchers are the MPs of all parties who are *not*:

	Labour	Conservative	Liberal Democrat
Women	101	13	3
Black and Asian	9	0	0
Professional	188	61	23
Business	37	65	11
Manual	54	1	1
Politics	40	15	5
Public school/non-Oxbridge degree	65	100	18
Oxbridge degree	61	84	15
Public school	67	109	19

Table 7.1 Backgrounds of MPs elected in 1997

- cabinet ministers
- members of the government
- members of the shadow cabinet
- part of the opposition's front-bench team

It is important to differentiate between the slightly differing roles of backbenchers from the government party and those from the opposition. Backbenchers from the government party are expected not to criticise the government too strongly, even when the interests of their constituents or constituency are at issue. Opposition backbenchers are expected to play a prominent part in opposing the government as well as looking after the interests of their constituency. Be aware of the debate about whether an MP should be a party delegate (and bound by party instructions) or a representative from his or her constituency. Representatives are supposed to be free agents who can judge each issue on its merits.

The main opportunities for backbenchers to represent their constituency and constituents in the House of Commons are as follows:

- Each parliamentary day usually opens with questions, which gives backbenchers of all parties the chance to question ministers.
- Backbenchers have the right to ask for a written answer to any question, and that answer is published in Hansard (the official record).
- Backbenchers have the right to participate in all debates on legislation.
- Backbenchers have the right to vote on all bills.
- Each parliamentary day ends with an adjournment debate, when a backbencher has the opportunity to debate an issue that affects his or her constituency with the relevant minister, who has to be present and respond to the backbencher.
- All the main parliamentary committees, such as standing committees on bills and the select departmental committees, as well as the key scrutiny committee, the Public Accounts Committee, are chaired by backbenchers and the whole of their membership is made up of backbenchers.
- Backbenchers can refer matters dealing with possible maladministration to the ombudsman (the parliamentary commissioner for administration).
- Backbenchers have the right to raise any matter affecting a constituency with any minister, in writing, and they are guaranteed a reply.

It is easy to find recent examples of the work of backbenchers using the House of Commons website. Make sure you know some examples of individual backbench success, as well as a success achieved by a group of backbenchers pressurising the government.

An impartial speaker is vital to the effective functioning of the Commons.

THE SPEAKER

The speaker of the House of Commons is always an MP of considerable seniority, elected by the other MPs. The speaker at the time of writing is Michael Martin. He has the responsibility of managing the House of Commons and acting as the MPs' spokesperson. He chairs all major debates (except for those on the Budget) and decides who may speak in which debates. He also has the role of keeping order in the House of Commons, and deciding whether to allow special emergency debates in the event of a crisis. The speaker has a vital role in ensuring that all MPs have the chance to speak, that the opposition gets the chance to criticise the government, and that minority parties can also play a role in parliament.

D The role of party

THE IMPORTANCE OF PARTIES

There is frequently a debate as to whether MPs are actually constituency **representatives** (agents who are free to vote as they see fit) or party **delegates** (committed to obeying party instructions). For most of the time, most MPs do as they are instructed by their parties, so party plays a huge role in parliament. MPs of all parties receive weekly instructions from their **whips** (party managers in parliament) telling them when and how to vote. The speaker will manage debates to ensure that there is fair representation from all parties. Committees of the House of Commons are always organised on party lines. It is loyalty to the party line that is most likely to ensure promotion to ministerial rank. Disloyalty to the party can lead to expulsion from the party, and thus an end to an MP's career in parliament. Party is the single most important factor influencing the conduct of all MPs.

THE NEED FOR PARTIES

Without party organisation and loyalty it would be very difficult for the government of the day to get major measures through parliament. There are about 100 members of the government in the House of Commons, who, if they disobey the whips, can expect to be sacked or have to resign, and thus lose their ministerial salary and chances of promotion. With about 650 MPs in total, this does not give the government a majority, so it needs the support of the other party members in the House of Commons to get potentially unpopular measures through. The whips argue that an MP is elected because of her or his party 'label', and therefore the first loyalty of the MP should be to the party in parliament. Some independent-minded MPs argue that they should have more freedom to vote according to their conscience or the needs of their constituents.

PARTY DISCIPLINE AND CONFLICTS OF LOYALTY

A major reason for the defeat of the Conservatives in the 1997 election was the open divisions between the Conservative government of John Major and many of his backbench MPs. As a result, Tony Blair and his whips maintained very tight discipline over Labour backbench MPs between 1997 and 2001 in order to maintain an appearance of unity, seen as vital for winning elections.

Be aware of the vital nature of the role of party in parliament, and be prepared also to debate the merits and demerits of it.

Consider the difficult position of a backbench Labour MP in 2001, who is a member of a select committee monitoring the performance of a government department. She feels that the minister (from the same party as hers) and the department he is in charge of have acted incompetently. Should she highlight this and embarrass the party of which she is a member, and the government of which she would love to be a member? This highlights the problems arising from the lack of separation of powers in the British system and the conflicting demands on MPs.

E   The role of the opposition

The opposition is given the opportunity to make its views known, and to criticise the government, in several ways:

- Opposition MPs can use Question Time and the adjournment debate to harass ministers.
- The leader of the opposition is always allowed to question the prime minister on a Wednesday.
- In any debate on a government bill, the speaker always looks to the shadow spokesperson (principal expert MP from the opposition party) to challenge the minister, and opposition MPs are given the chance to speak later in the debate.
- The opposition may vote against a bill.
- Opposition MPs are on all committees of the Commons, both standing and select (but they are always in a minority).
- The opposition is given about 20 days a year to raise issues for debate. The opposition chooses the topic, and the relevant ministers have to be there to have their policies criticised and defend them. A good recent example arose in July 2001 when the opposition strongly criticised the government over the introduction of the new AS examinations. The secretary of state for education, Estelle Morris, had to attend the debate to defend the government's policy, explain that she had ordered an inquiry into the whole system, report on the results of the inquiry and indicate what changes would be made.

Look up the education debate from July 2001 on the House of Commons website — it is a good example of the work of opposition.

The opposition has plenty of scope to criticise the government, but it has limited potential to achieve much else if the government of the day has a reliable majority.

F   How laws are made

A major part of the work of parliament lies in making legislation. This legislation can be of vital national importance (e.g. a law to take the UK into the European Union) or it can be a minor matter (e.g. a law dealing with the labelling of Scotch whisky) which affects only a few people.

There are two main types of legislation:

- The vast majority of laws are **government bills** put forward by the government of the day.
- Other laws are put forward by ordinary backbench MPs — these are called **Private Members' bills**.

Look up the Queen's Speech on parliament's website.

GOVERNMENT BILLS

A **bill** is a proposal for legislation put to parliament. Ministers often request more bills than there is parliamentary time for, so a cabinet committee decides which bills will go before parliament in the coming session and their order of priority. Clearly the prime minister will have a lot of influence over this.

- **Queen's Speech.** The bills are then listed in the Queen's Speech, which is written for the queen by Number 10. It is then the job of the leaders of the House of Commons and Lords (both members of the cabinet) and the whips to get the bills through parliament. Note the way in which this process is dominated by the government. This shows very clearly how the executive dominates parliament.

- **First reading.** This means the simple announcement to the House of Commons that a bill on a particular subject (e.g. the compulsory wearing of seatbelts) is coming. Printed copies of the bill are made available for everyone to scrutinise. This gives pressure groups and other opponents or supporters of the bill the opportunity to study it, to get organised and to brief MPs for or against it.

- **Second reading.** This is the most important stage in the passage of a bill, usually taking place a few weeks after the formal first reading. The relevant minister (the transport minister in the case of seatbelts) will introduce the bill and argue for its support. The opposition spokesperson and backbenchers are then given ample opportunity to debate the measure, and at the end of the day a vote is taken. If it succeeds, this means that the House accepts the bill in principle. In the case of a normal bill, MPs will usually follow their party instructions on how to vote. When the government has a majority, a government bill invariably passes. There is limited scope for the opposition or backbenchers to achieve much in the way of preventing a bill or amending it if the government has a reliable majority who obey the whips.

The most likely area to be questioned is the effectiveness of the Commons as a legislative body. Consider ways in which law making could be improved.

- **Committee stage.** The bill then goes to a standing committee — a group of backbench MPs whose role is to examine the bill in detail and make any necessary changes (e.g. allowing milk delivery people not to put on a seatbelt every time they get into their vans). It is usual for the principles behind the bill to remain unchanged. The majority of the committee are always members of the party of government, and the chair of the committee is also a member of the majority party in the Commons. On the whole, they do as the whips tell them. This is another example of the way in which the executive dominates parliament. It is argued that parliament cannot do its job of legislating properly with the whips so obviously 'on'.

  MPs on the standing committee may not have any expertise in the relevant area; nor are they paid extra for such work. Although committee work is vital to improve bills, which may have been drawn up hurriedly, little status is given to such work by MPs and it is unlikely to improve their chances of promotion. Moreover, standing committees do not have the additional resources that their counterparts in the EU or the USA enjoy to carry out detailed research on bills and to question ministers and civil servants on them.

- **Report stage.** If major changes are made by the standing committee then the House of Commons has to agree to them. A government with a majority invariably gets its way.

- **Third reading.** This is usually just a formality and there is no debate.

- **Lords and royal assent.** The bill must then be dealt with by the House of Lords and approved by the monarch before it becomes the law of the land. The House of Lords can be a major obstacle to the passage of a bill.

PRIVATE MEMBERS' BILLS

Every year in parliament a certain amount of time is set aside for legislation put forward by ordinary backbenchers. As so many wish to put forward a bill, those who are allowed to use the limited time available are chosen by ballot, and not on grounds of importance. Some very important laws, such as the abolition of capital punishment, permitting homosexual acts and major changes in the divorce law have taken this route.

Governments prefer to avoid introducing legislation like this, as they can tend to lose the government party votes in subsequent elections. However, Private Members' bills can be very difficult to pass and are easy to block. For example, a bill to ban hunting with dogs was lost despite widespread support in the Commons and outside parliament. Many feel that important issues such as those mentioned above should not be so dependent on the luck of a ballot and limited parliamentary time.

The main criticisms of Private Members' bills are as follows:
- They are chosen by ballot and not by importance.
- Major measures should not just be left to chance.
- Parliament should play a greater role in setting its own agenda.
- Although there are technically 'free' votes on such bills, the government and its whips are not averse to putting pressure on MPs to vote in a particular way.
- Such bills are easy to destroy on technicalities.
- They tend to be heard on a Friday when many MPs have returned to their constituencies.

G The role of standing and select committees

STANDING COMMITTEES

These are groups of backbench MPs who have the role of examining a bill in detail. Bills come to a standing committee after they have passed their second reading. Although no member of the government may be a member, there is always a government majority on the committee and the chair is also a member of the majority party. It is very unusual for a standing committee to make any significant changes to the principles behind a bill, but it may make many **amendments** (changes). It may call the relevant ministers or civil servants to explain items, and it may occasionally call outside experts. The whips are 'on', so the government almost invariably gets its way. If the government is in a hurry, it is possible to cut short the discussion in committee by use of a procedural device called a **guillotine**, even when only a small amount of the bill has been examined. The bill is then returned to the Commons for the report stage and the third reading.

Look at the House of Commons website and see what types of bill were put forward by backbenchers in the previous session of parliament and which ones, if any, were successful.

The actual value of the work of a standing committee can be very limited.

SELECT COMMITTEES

Gladstone created the first select committee, the Public Accounts Committee, in the 1860s. Select committees are groups of backbenchers who have a responsibility for examining the work of a department, such as the Home Office, or for looking at a specific area, such as the ombudsman, or the public accounts.

Again, no member of the government may be a member, but most of the MPs on the committee will be from the majority party, and the majority party will also provide most of the chairs of the committees.

Their main aim is to provide a means of scrutinising the government and other public institutions, such as the television companies and the railways, and of upholding the public interest.

MERITS OF SELECT COMMITTEES

They have the right to request ministers and civil servants to appear before them, and the evidence that they give is, of course, televised and reported. Naturally, ministers and civil servants do not wish to appear incompetent in front of parliament and the cameras, so they keep on their toes. Committees can also highlight deficiencies in government, and focus the attention of government on real problems. Examples of where select committees have encouraged government to act are:
- the safety of RoRo ferries
- caring for Gulf War veterans suffering from 'Gulf War Syndrome'
- providing sufficient customs officers at some ports to prevent drug smuggling
- ensuring a reduction in number of deaths in police custody on Saturday nights
- highlighting the Bank of England's failure to regulate small banks when Barings and the BCCI Bank collapsed, ruining many investors

DEMERITS OF SELECT COMMITTEES

The main failing of select committees is that the majority of MPs on them are members of the same party as the government of the day, and they are bound to have difficulty in criticising government measures openly. These committees also do not have the power to *compel* ministers or civil servants to attend, answer questions or provide information. They have no power over legislation — they can point out failings, but they cannot enforce solutions. They do not have the resources to call on experts. Really able MPs are not interested in working for them, as they do not lead to becoming a minister. No additional pay is given to an MP who chooses to sit on a select committee. There was strong criticism of the government in 2001 when it tried to prevent potential critics within its own party from sitting on select committees.

THE PUBLIC ACCOUNTS COMMITTEE

Perhaps the most influential of the select committees is the Public Accounts Committee, which is always chaired by a senior member of the opposition. This committee has the power to summon civil servants and make them answer for the spending of their department. It has the support of the National Audit Office, which employs a large number of skilled accountants and, with its reports and investigative capacity, ensures minimal dishonesty and incompetence in British government.

You should know the reasoning behind select committees and their membership — they are one of the principal methods through which parliament can scrutinise the executive.

'Roll-on and roll-off' car ferries.

The actual workings of all committees can be seen on the House of Commons website, and you should look up your own examples.

H The scrutiny role of the House of Commons

It is important to emphasise the main methods by which the Commons can scrutinise or check the actions of the government. These are:

- questions — written and oral
- debates, such as adjournment debates at the end of each day
- motions of no-confidence
- standing committees
- select committees
- letters to ministers
- referring matters to the ombudsman

Many of these areas have already been described, so we will concentrate here on the roles of parliamentary questions and debates, and of the parliamentary commissioner for administration.

QUESTIONS AND DEBATES

Each main parliamentary day starts with questions to ministers. The normal procedure is for two ministers to be questioned every day. MPs put down their questions in advance, but are allowed to ask a supplementary or additional question. Ministers are obliged to attend and deal with issues relating to their department, and accept responsibility for it. The requirement to answer questions makes a minister keep fully up to date with the main work of the department, as the supplementary question is usually designed by opposition backbenchers to try and catch the minister out in public.

Ensure that you know some examples and can comment upon the effectiveness of both questions and debates in parliament.

There are also many opportunities for debates. Each bill is debated comprehensively in its second reading, and further debates take place when the opposition uses its time to debate an aspect of government policy (e.g. the government's foreign policy). Remember also that each day ends with an adjournment debate, when an MP can raise a matter that affects his or her constituency with a minister. There can be emergency debates during times of crisis, as happened following the terrorist attacks in New York and Washington in September 2001.

THE OMBUDSMAN

Examples of the ombudsman's successes — and there are few — can be gained from his website. But the limits to his powers also need to be known.

Known formally as the parliamentary commissioner for administration, the ombudsman was intended to be the means by which ordinary citizens could get redress of their grievances against an incompetent executive (e.g. quickly retrieving an overpayment of tax). However, the civil service managed to reduce the powers that it was proposed to give the ombudsman, and grievances can only be referred to the ombudsman through an MP. Even then the ombudsman has very limited powers to investigate complaints, punish incompetence or even compensate citizens who have been unfairly treated. The office is generally felt to be a waste of public money.

▌ Some important issues

The democratic implications of increasing executive domination of parliament need to be known.

THE EXECUTIVE'S DOMINATION OF PARLIAMENT

This currently manifests itself in several ways:

- With a large majority in the House of Commons, the present government appears to be able to win every vote it wishes.
- There is a majority of Labour MPs on every standing and select committee. Moreover, select committees have limited power and the ombudsman is powerless.
- The level of attendance of the prime minister and senior ministers in parliament is much lower than was the case in the 1980s. Tony Blair has reduced prime minister's Question Time from twice a week to once a week.

PARLIAMENT AND THE EU

It is vital to remember here that in many areas of public life the ability of parliament to make laws, particularly over trade, industry and agriculture, has been transferred to Europe.

Parliament has both select and standing committees which look at new legislation coming from Brussels, but there is limited interest in their work and they do not have the power to stop a European decision being implemented, unless the UK leaves the EU.

Parliament could exercise greater scrutiny over European decisions if it wished, but it prefers not to. Most parliaments in other EU member countries choose to exercise much tighter control over what the EU is doing than the British Parliament does. Most of the scrutiny role is delegated to the House of Lords.

Both devolution and the development of the EU have significantly limited the role of parliament.

PARLIAMENT AND DEVOLUTION

Similarly, with the passage of devolution for Scotland, Wales and Northern Ireland, certain powers are no longer managed by the Westminster Parliament, but are devolved to the national assemblies and parliament (e.g. education in Scotland). This has led to a further reduction in the sovereignty of the UK Parliament.

REFORM OF THE HOUSE OF COMMONS

Many reforms have been suggested for the House of Commons. Ones that have been considered recently are:

- working more normal hours, with no more late-night sittings
- reforming the method by which MPs are elected to ensure they reflect the popular vote
- ensuring that more women/ethnic minority MPs are elected
- giving select committees more power to scrutinise the executive
- giving more power to standing committees to modify or improve legislation
- giving more scope for Private Members' bills, and changing the way in which they are chosen
- giving parliament greater control over European legislation
- tightening ethical standards for MPs — there have been several strong complaints about corruption amongst MPs

- giving more technical and research support to MPs, so that they can scrutinise ministers better

J Key terms and concepts

Delegates and representatives It is part of the constitutional process in the UK that MPs are representatives and not delegates. A representative is chosen by the constituency to go to Westminster and take decisions on behalf of the electorate. An MP is expected to listen to constituents, but still exercise her or his own judgement. If a local referendum were 100% in favour of legalising cannabis, a 'representative' MP would still be entitled to vote against it if the MP felt that it was the right decision. However, if an MP were seen as a delegate, then the MP would be bound to follow the instructions of his or her constituents. Make sure you are clear about the difference between the two terms.

Fusion of powers This occurs when the three key parts of the state — executive, legislature and judiciary — are all integrated, as they are in the UK. The prime minister and other ministers are all members of both the executive and the legislature (i.e. they are ministers and MPs), while the Lord Chancellor is involved with all three powers. Some writers argue that, because powers are fused, the UK is not a very democratic society.

Parliamentary government This is achieved when parliament is the most powerful element in government and dominates the executive. All ministers must be members of parliament and they are primarily accountable to parliament.

Presidential government Modern prime ministers, particularly Margaret Thatcher and Tony Blair, are increasingly accused of acting 'presidentially'. This means that parliament is no longer the focal point of government; instead the focus has gone to the executive, and particularly to the head of the executive — the prime minister.

Public accountability Parliament is the main route through which the public can call the government to account, examine and criticise its actions and, if necessary (as in 1979), dismiss a government that it feels is failing.

Representative government A system of government where the electorate has given an elected parliament the power to take the major decisions on its behalf. Under this system, a decision to legalise cannabis would be taken by MPs and peers, not by the electorate as a whole. The growing use of the referendum, where citizens are consulted directly, obviously works against representative government.

Separation of powers This occurs when all three parts of the state — executive, legislature and judiciary — are totally separate, as in the USA. No one may be a member of more than one power. A minister in the USA cannot be both a member of Congress and a judge. This is designed to protect the democratic process so that every power is checked and balanced by the others.

As with the House of Commons, the House of Lords is a central topic with all three examination boards at AS. It is a topic where it is particularly important to ensure that a recent textbook is used, as there have been major changes since 1997. There is also a strong likelihood of further major changes in the coming years. Many of the facts and ideas below could come up as direct questions on the House of Lords, but they could also come up in other questions, such as on Labour Party policy or the constitution. The best way to find out about all the major changes in detail, and also about the day-to-day operation of the Lords, is to visit the House of Lords section of the parliament website.

Key questions

What is the present role of the House of Lords?

How important are the recent reforms of the House of Lords?

Is the House of Lords still appropriate in a democracy?

Does the UK need a second chamber?

A Development of the House of Lords

One of the earliest roles of the Lords was that of a conservative body which supported the monarch.

EARLY DEVELOPMENTS

Originally the House of Lords was one of three Houses of Parliament. At the end of the fifteenth century it merged with the House of Clergy. From 1500 onwards it had equal status to the House of Commons, although it was smaller and its members were not elected. Membership was either by inheriting a title, such as an earldom, or being made a peer by the monarch. As early as the sixteenth century, however, it was the elected House of Commons that tended to take the initiative against the monarch in matters of policy, with the Lords being a much more conservative body that tended to support the monarch. This role lasted well into the nineteenth century.

Refusal to adhere to constitutional convention in the nineteenth century led to the House of Lords' power being radically reduced.

CHANGES IN THE NINETEENTH AND TWENTIETH CENTURIES

By the end of the nineteenth century, the House of Lords was playing a minor role in government. Convention was that it should play no part in money bills, and just agree to what the democratically elected House of Commons wished. When it came to non-money bills, the convention was that if the government of the day had a clear **mandate** for a bill (it had been in the governing party's manifesto and it had then won an election), the House of Lords should allow the Commons bill to pass, after due deliberation. However, when the Lords rejected Home Rule for Ireland in the 1890s, for which the government had a clear mandate, and also rejected a Budget in 1909, they had to be reformed.

REFORM OF THE HOUSE OF LORDS IN THE TWENTIETH CENTURY

The first major reform of the Lords was the Parliament Act of 1911. This prevented the Lords exercising a **veto** (the ability to reject) on any money bill, and only allowed the Lords to delay other bills for three **sessions** (years) of parliament. There was no change to the membership of the Lords, which remained made up of hereditary peers, bishops of the Church of England (not Catholics) and the Law Lords.

The House of Lords gradually became a less undemocratic and less unrepresentative institution in the twentieth century.

The delaying power was further reduced in the Parliament Act of 1949, to one session. Other changes included the Life Peerage Act of 1958, which gave the prime minister the power to give people of either sex the right to sit and vote in the Lords in their own lifetime. The titles of these life peers did not pass down to the eldest son. An act of 1963 gave hereditary peers the right to give up their hereditary peerages.

B The present composition of the House of Lords

Until 1998 there were several different types of member of the House of Lords:
- There were about 634 **hereditary peers**, who held their seats there because they had inherited a title. Many of these did not use their right to sit, vote and debate in the Lords.
- There were 479 **life peers**, who included women. These also included the **Law Lords** — the top judges — who had taken over the old judicial functions of the House of Lords.
- There were 26 Church of England **bishops and archbishops**.

Note the clear breach of the 'separation of powers' concept here.

They were presided over by the lord chancellor, who was also a member of the cabinet.

About 474 of the total of 1,139 peers were Conservative supporters, and 156 Labour.

The House of Lords is still at present an appointive body. No members are elected.

In the recent Labour government reforms, the right of the hereditary peers to sit, debate and vote was abolished. A few hereditary peers remain until a further major reform of the Lords takes place. The prime minister can create new members.

C The present role of the House of Lords

Given the fact that there is no written constitution that specifies the role of the Lords, custom plays a part. It ought to be stressed that different writers might advocate different views here. However, the main functions of this second chamber are probably as follows:
- **To scrutinise the work of the executive.** The Lords has a Question Time and every government department has one peer linked to it who will answer questions.
- **To debate bills.** All bills have to be passed by both the Lords and the Commons.

Look at the Lords' work
on the latest bill to ban
hunting with hounds.

- **To revise bills carefully.** Sometimes the House of Commons may not have had time to deal with a bill properly. The Lords have been known to make dozens of major amendments to bills to improve them. Pressure groups often rely on the Lords to make changes to bills, as they often cannot get access to Commons standing committees.
- **To delay bills.** The Lords may feel that a particular proposal is wrong or unnecessary and may therefore act to delay its passage. This is an area where the Lords most often come into conflict with the government, as the Lords are accused of holding up the will of the elected part of the constitution. This ability to delay is one of the main reasons why the present government is reluctant to give more power to the House of Lords. The lack of power in the Lords is probably a major reason why many people do not want to become members of it.
- **To check a government.** A government that had a majority in the Commons would be able to steamroller its programme through without the power of the Lords to stop it.
- **To deal with non-controversial matters.** Many non-controversial issues require legislation, and the involvement of the Lords saves the Commons a lot of time.
- **To examine bills and debate policy in a non-partisan manner.** Although many of the members of the Lords take a party whip, there are few ways in which they can be disciplined for disobeying it; many others do not take a whip; and since all peers have no electors to worry about, they are in a position to speak and vote freely.
- **To debate major and controversial issues.** The Lords can debate controversial subjects such as genetic engineering and the age of consent without concern for political parties or the electorate. The House of Commons is often worried about debating such issues, as MPs fear that what they say might offend their electors or their party bosses.
- **To debate and examine European legislation.** The House of Commons does not seem to wish to undertake the detailed examination of EU legislation.
- **To provide ministers.** The Lords is able to provide the government with ministers who do not have to worry about constituents (e.g. Lord Falconer, the minister for the 'Dome' in the Labour government of 1997–2001). This is a good way of bringing possible talent into the government.

D Criticisms of the House of Lords

All the major criticisms
of the old Lords need
learning — and be
prepared to comment
on whether Tony Blair's
reforms (see page 67)
are an improvement.

Several criticisms were levelled at the unreformed House of Lords. There were criticisms of both the membership and the role.

- The main criticism was the method of selection. Simply because your grandfather had the cash to buy a peerage from Lloyd George in 1921, or your great-grandfather was a brilliant general, was no reason why you should be in the Lords. Also, being a man's eldest son is not a good criterion.
- The system seemed to be both racist and sexist, with few women or members of ethnic minorities.

- There were Church of England bishops, but no Catholic bishops or elders of any other religious faith, so selection for the Lords discriminated on religious grounds as well.
- The Conservatives tended to dominate, and many of the hereditary peers only came to the Lords when requested to by the Conservative whips to vote for Conservative measures.
- The Lords did not seem to do much. They seemed relatively powerless, and the bulk of their work was doing things that the House of Commons should really have been doing.
- Peers were not paid, but they received quite a generous attendance allowance and expenses if they turned up. They did not have to vote, speak or actually take part in any way, in order to receive these payments.

E Reform of the House of Lords

All attempts to modernise the Lords in the 1960s and 1970s failed.

Attempts were made to reform the Lords in both the 1960s (the Crossman reforms) and 1970s (the Home reforms), but they broke down for several reasons:

- No one could agree, first, on whether reform was actually needed and, second, on whether it was just the membership of the Lords that needed to change or its role as well.
- There was also no consensus about whether peers should be elected or appointed.
- The House of Commons was very reluctant to give up any power, and the executive was reluctant to change any system in a way that might reduce its powers.
- It occurred to some that if you started to get rid of the hereditary principle behind much of the membership of the House of Lords, the idea might catch on with the monarchy as well.
- The changes would have to be written down in an act of parliament, and logic might then dictate that a written constitution had to be produced which covered everything else.

HOUSE OF LORDS ACT, 1999

The Labour government elected in 1997 was committed to the reform of the House of Lords. It was a major item in the party's manifesto. On election, the prime minister set up a cabinet committee, chaired by the lord chancellor, Lord Irvine, to recommend reforms. There was some concern that the reform of the Lords had been given to its most important member and speaker, and that 'outsiders' might bring a more democratic approach to bear.

The first result was the 1999 House of Lords Act, which:

- removed the right of the hereditary peers to sit and vote in the Lords, with the exception of 92 'transition' hereditary peers, who would be elected by the other departing hereditary peers. These transition peers would gradually be phased out entirely

- left 527 life peers, who would make up the main membership of the reformed House of Lords
- left the 26 bishops and archbishops of the Church of England and 27 Law Lords

THE WAKEHAM COMMISSION

The Labour government then set up a royal commission to investigate the whole issue and recommend changes. A royal commission is a group of individuals, chosen by the government, who are given the role of investigating an issue and recommending policy changes. It is customary for a government to take very seriously the recommendations of a royal commission and make them law.

This royal commission was chaired by Lord Wakeham, a life peer who had been a senior minister under Margaret Thatcher in the 1980s. There was strong criticism from those who wished for a radical change because both the chairman and the members of the royal commission were very 'conservative' types, chosen because they were unlikely to recommend anything radical. The commission was asked to examine both the role and the membership of the House of Lords. When it published its report in 2000, it made the following recommendations:

- The changed House of Lords should bring experience and expertise, in areas such as agriculture, the armed services, social services and business, to the political process.
- It should be more representative, meaning that it should represent different social, ethnic and regional groups. This also implied that there should be an elected element.
- It should reflect the views of the regions of England and the nations of Scotland, Wales and Northern Ireland. Care should be taken to ensure that residents of those areas were in the Lords.
- It should help to check the executive — but the report was very vague about how this could or should be done.
- It should be largely appointive, chosen by the prime minister or by an independent group. This inevitably caused major debate.
- There should be some elected members, but they should be a minority. The majority should be appointed.
- It should not be dominated by parties. It was hoped to develop a much more non-partisan atmosphere in the Lords, so that issues and bills could be looked at on their merits and not as a means of scoring points against another party.
- There should be no increase in the powers of the Lords. Inevitably this raised the issue of whether able men and women would wish to become members if they did not have the prospect of exercising much influence.
- Members should hold their seats for terms of 15 years, not for life.
- Religions in addition to the Church of England should be represented. In an increasingly secular age and an increasingly multi-faith society, this caused debate over which religions.
- The Lords should have a particular brief for civil liberties. This was a popular suggestion, but what it actually meant in practice was not explained. No additional powers were to be given which might help it to achieve a greater focus on civil liberties in the UK.

Several criticisms of the recommendations have been made:

- The members of the royal commission were reluctant to change the powers of the House of Lords and wished to see the continuing dominance of the House of Commons and the executive in the whole political process.
- There will be a minority of elected members in the Lords.
- There is no mechanism for further scrutiny of the government.
- Given the scope of the changes it is felt that there will be little change in the British constitutional process.
- The appointments made by the prime minister and the leader of the opposition have indicated that they wish to have the same type of person in the House of Lords as has been the case with life peers in the past.

A very likely question is whether the House of Lords still needs further reform.

F Key terms and concepts

Democracy A system of government where citizens are involved in choosing a representative from competing political parties to make decisions on their behalf. As citizens have no choice in the selection of members of the House of Lords, its 'undemocratic' nature is obvious. It could be argued, however, that if the Lords were a more representative institution in terms of gender, race, region and occupation than the House of Commons, it might come to be seen as a 'democratic' institution.

Hereditary peers Noblemen who gained their titles and seats in the House of Lords by inheriting their title (e.g. Duke of Westminster) from their father or another relative. The title gave its holder the right to sit and vote in the House of Lords. It was not necessary to be either able or elected by the people.

This is a major topic and the likelihood of a compulsory question on it is high. Candidates are strongly advised to look at media reports on the annual conferences of the three major parties that have taken place during their period of study; to look carefully at all major government policy initiatives, such as the Budget; and to be aware of the principal policies of the government of the day and the opposition's reactions to those policies. If there has been major disagreement within a party over an issue, such as the backbench revolt by Labour MPs over the Labour government's proposed privatisation of the air traffic control system, this should be known. You will not stand a chance of the top grade unless there is recent and accurate knowledge of party policies and developments.

Key questions

What are the roles and functions of political parties?

What are the main policies and ideologies of the principal political parties?

How democratic are the main political parties in their structure and organisation?

How do the main political parties select their candidates and leaders?

How is policy made in the main political parties?

What is the role of the ordinary member in political parties?

How are parties financed?

Where does power lie in modern political parties?

A The Conservative Party

ORIGINS AND DEVELOPMENT

The modern Conservative Party dates from the 1830s, when Robert Peel persuaded the old Tory Party to adopt the name of 'Conservative' together with new policies and important organisational changes. In the past, the Tory Party had opposed any change at all. Peel also persuaded it to broaden its membership to include more than just aristocrats and landed gentry, and to appeal to the growing middle class — Peel himself was the son of a successful manufacturer.

The change from Tory to Conservative led to the Conservatives becoming a much more flexible and pragmatic party.

In the course of the nineteenth century, the Conservative Party went through periods of 'conservatism', where it opposed the more radical Liberals and their desire for change, but there were several periods in the nineteenth century when the Conservative Party put major political, social and economic change through parliament. In 1867 it was a Conservative government that actually gave the urban working class the right to vote. In the 1870s it was another Conservative government that started a programme of radical social reform which improved working and living conditions for the working class.

By 1900 the Conservative Party had a record of being flexible and adaptable with its policies, and being capable of radical changes.

THE MODERN CONSERVATIVE PARTY

In the course of the twentieth century, the Conservative Party retained its record for adapting to change. One of the first industries to be nationalised in the 1920s, electricity, was nationalised by the Conservatives. However, it was also the same Conservative government that broke the General Strike in 1926 and penalised the trade unions involved.

It was a Conservative government that took the UK into the EU (then the EEC) in 1972, and the Conservative governments of the 1951–64 period that accepted nationalised industries and the National Health Service. Margaret Thatcher in the 1980s also put forward radical reforms affecting education, the health service, the civil service, local government and the trade unions, and privatised many nationalised industries. With the Single European Act of 1986, Margaret Thatcher was responsible for integrating the UK much more into the EU.

The tradition of moving between conservatism and radicalism is a theme in Conservative Party development.

The party remains willing to be both 'conservative' (in cutting public spending and allowing private schools and medicine to develop) and radical.

THE CONSERVATIVE PARTY UNDER WILLIAM HAGUE

You need a reasonable knowledge of William Hague's changes to the party structure as well as to party policy between 1997 and 2001. The main ideas and record of his successor will also need to be known by June 2002. The main changes to the party introduced by William Hague are as follows:

- Ordinary party members were allowed to vote for the leader. This happened in the selection of the replacement for William Hague. Conservative MPs narrowed down the candidates to two, and party members then chose one to lead them. Since the 1960s it had only been Conservative MPs who could vote for their leader.
- A written party constitution was introduced. Until then the Conservative Party had managed without one. Leaders preferred it this way, as it enabled them to make the rules, which made them more powerful within the party.
- A national membership scheme was introduced to increase party membership and income. There were concerns that membership was falling and becoming increasingly elderly. There was a real shortage of party activists who would help at elections.
- There was greater involvement by party members in policy making through the Policy Forum. In the past, although there was some scope for members to give their views on policy at conference and through their MPs, there was no formal way of doing this.

It is common for a party suffering a major defeat in an election (like Labour in 1979 and 1983) to embark on major internal change as well as find a new leader.

These changes, proposed in 1998 in a document called *The Fresh Future*, were approved in a vote of party members by 96% of those who took part (there was a 33% turnout). This consultation and more democratic approach continued with a referendum on Conservative policy on the euro. A majority of 84% of party members backed William Hague's policy of opposing it (on a 60% turnout).

The easiest way to see Conservative policies for yourself, and not through the eyes of a possibly biased journalist, is to look at the party's own website. The most important areas to consider are:

- taxation
- public spending

- defence, especially the idea of a 'European' force
- health care
- the European Union, and the euro in particular
- the role of government
- law and order and policing issues
- attitudes to immigration and asylum seekers

Some commentators argue that William Hague moved the party much more to the right.

KEY POINTS IN THE CONSERVATIVE MANIFESTO, 2001

Although it is extremely likely that the new leader of the Conservative Party, Iain Duncan Smith, will change party policy in the next few years, a working knowledge of current 'Conservatism' is required. The main policies in the Conservative manifesto of 2001 (entitled *Time for Common Sense*) were:

- £8 billion of tax cuts, funded by cutting down on social security fraud and 'slimming down' government departments. One of the biggest tax cuts was to be 6p off a litre of petrol
- deregulation for business — cutting 'red tape'
- greater scope for individual schools to act independently of local authorities
- more police, more prisons and tougher prison sentences
- matching Labour's spending on health and pensions
- tightening the regulations on asylum seekers
- opposing the euro, renegotiating the Treaty of Nice, opposing the European Rapid Reaction Force and changing the Common Agricultural Policy. The whole tenor of the manifesto was very hostile to the EU

Commentators felt that the Conservative manifesto did not offer a radical alternative to what the Labour Party was offering. There were no fundamental differences on most major issues. The biggest difference between the two parties lay in their attitudes to the EU, but even the Conservatives did not wish to leave it.

B The Labour Party

ORIGINS AND DEVELOPMENT

The Labour Party was created mainly by:

- the trade unions, which provided the money and the voters
- middle-class intellectuals, who added much in the way of a socialist ideology and organisational skills

Although a Labour government was in office in the 1920s and 1930s, it never had a majority and therefore was unable to get through much of the legislation it wanted. Labour's first majority government took office between 1945 and 1951 — a period marked by the creation of the welfare state and the National Health Service, and a major programme of nationalising strategic industries. The country recovered well after a devastating war, and by the time Labour left office it had attained full employment, achieved a balance of international payments and created a welfare state.

Do not get too immersed in Labour's history.

The first period in office of a majority Labour government was marked by huge changes in the welfare state.

During the period 1951–79, when the Labour Party was in office it tended to have very similar policies to the Conservatives. On the main areas such as the role of the government in managing the economy, foreign policy, and even public spending and taxation, there was no real disagreement between the two parties. It is worth noting that Labour was split on entry into the EU (then the EEC) in 1972, and that the Conservatives (also badly split) only passed the act to join the EU with the support of Labour MPs. The Conservatives who supported the EU returned the favour in 1975, when many Conservative MPs supported the Labour government in the referendum campaign to stay in the EU, even appearing on the same platform as Labour ministers.

> There were no real differences in policy between Labour and the Conservatives in the period 1950–79, and both parties split over Europe in the 1960s and 1970s.

THE MODERN LABOUR PARTY
In 1979 the Labour Party under James Callaghan lost the election to the Conservatives under Margaret Thatcher. The party then moved very firmly for the first time in a markedly socialist direction. Under the leadership of Michael Foot and Tony Benn, not only was power in the party pushed very much down to the grassroots, but policies became much more socialist. Many members and MPs, including key former ministers such as Roy Jenkins, left to form a new party, the Social Democratic Party (since merged with the Liberals to form the Liberal Democrats).

In its 1983 manifesto, the Labour Party advocated:
- leaving NATO
- leaving the EU
- abolishing private medicine and private education
- giving up the nuclear deterrent
- hugely increasing nationalisation of finance and industry
- considerably increasing taxation and public spending

These left-wing ideas played an important part in Labour's massive defeat in the election of 1983 and the manifesto was nicknamed 'the longest suicide note in history'. The Liberals and Social Democrats between them obtained nearly as many votes as the Labour Party did. It was a humiliating defeat for the Labour Party, and its chances of ever returning to power were seen as very thin (in contrast with the Conservatives in 1997 and 2001).

> Many commentators feel that the adoption of very left-wing policies by the Labour Party in 1983 led to its defeat in the elections of 1983 and 1987.

THE LEADERSHIP OF NEIL KINNOCK AND TONY BLAIR, 1983–97
As a result of the defeat in the elections of 1979 and 1983 (and a further one in 1987), the Labour Party was prepared to introduce changes in its policies and organisation in order to make it capable of winning elections and forming a government. It became very clear in the course of the 1980s that many British voters broadly approved of what the Conservatives under Margaret Thatcher were doing, and that unless the Labour Party adapted and took on board some of her ideas, it would remain in opposition.

The main changes in Labour Party organisation and policy in this period were as follows:
- The role and power of the trade unions within the party was reduced. Margaret Thatcher's policy of reducing trade union influence was very popular with the British public.

- The Labour Party's reliance on the trade unions for funding was also reduced. Money would have to be gained from other sources — by attracting individual rich donors and increasing ordinary membership.
- The leader's power over membership, candidate selection, party structure and policy making was increased. This would enable the party to adopt more moderate policies that would appeal to the 'middle ground' of electors, who had deserted the Labour Party very obviously in the 1983 elections.
- The influence of radical socialist groups such as the Militant Tendency in the party was ended, and their hold over local government in areas such as London and Liverpool was destroyed. The damaging media portrayal of the work of party members such as Derek Hatton in Liverpool and Ken Livingstone in London was seen as having driven away traditional Labour voters.
- The party moved much further to the right to win over middle-income and middle-class voters. With class realignment taking place on a very large scale, traditional working-class Labour voters were now a much smaller part of the electorate. If Labour advocated policies that only appealed to this decreasing proportion of the population, it would never regain power.
- The party abandoned its traditional 'tax and spend' policies. The public clearly liked Margaret Thatcher's reductions in direct taxation — particularly income tax — and would not vote for a Labour Party that advocated an increase in taxation.
- It accepted the popular privatisation programmes of the Conservatives. A very large number of potential Labour voters had bought shares in newly privatised industries such as gas and telecommunications. Also many potential Labour voters had bought their former council houses.
- The party accepted the idea of devolution for Scotland, Northern Ireland and Wales, which James Callaghan and 'Old Labour' had been very hostile to.
- It accepted membership of the EU and NATO — in fact, it became enthusiastic about membership of both.
- It accepted the existence of private health care and private schools. Several major trade unions had actually negotiated agreements for their members with large employers, which included membership of private health schemes.

The changes introduced by Blair and Kinnock represent a major shift in the policies and possibly also in the ideology of the Labour Party.

The party leadership referred to the changed party as 'New Labour' to make it clear that there was a real distance between it and the 'Old' Labour Party of 1983 which had proved so unpopular with the electorate. Many of the changes were the work of Neil Kinnock, the Labour leader until 1992, when the Labour Party narrowly lost the election of that year. The changes in the Labour Party are seen by many commentators as a remarkable achievement on his part, and one of his key aides in the process of 'modernising' the party was Tony Blair.

THE LABOUR PARTY IN GOVERNMENT, 1997–2001

The Labour Party's website explains what Tony Blair is trying to achieve with his 'Third Way' between Old Labour's socialism and the free-market ideas of Margaret Thatcher. The main areas to look at are as follows:

- public spending
- taxation
- health and education
- the Bank of England

- the Social Chapter
- the Human Rights Act
- devolution to Wales, Scotland and Northern Ireland
- the Northern Ireland peace process
- the 'Welfare to Work' programme
- reform of the House of Lords
- benefits and pensions
- the euro
- ethical foreign policy
- intervention in Kosovo
- 'war on terrorism'

Consider whether Tony Blair has had as major an impact on the Labour Party as Neil Kinnock.

You should be able to work out for yourself how 'new' is New Labour, and how it might differ from Old Labour. Tony Blair has continued to ensure that the party leader remains firmly in control of party policy and candidate selection.

THE LABOUR PARTY MANIFESTO, 2001

A detailed working knowledge of the 44-page, 28,000-word document is not required, but knowledge of the key points is, in order to deal with questions on party policy and ideology, and also with questions on the general election of 2001. It is worth noting that the manifesto contained seven photographs of Tony Blair, and none of any other Labour politician.

The main points in the manifesto, entitled *Ambitions for Britain*, were:
- opposition to any increase in income tax
- support for the EU and promise of a referendum on the euro
- more teachers, doctors and nurses, and a willingness to work with the private sector in both health and education to improve services — education was the 'number one priority'
- £180 billion investment in road and rail improvement
- more police and a tougher stance on law and order
- extension of the 'Welfare to Work' programme — 'The Benefits System will be restructured around work'
- a tougher line on asylum seekers
- minor constitutional changes to the House of Lords and a 'possible review' of proportional representation by 2003

Commentators did not feel that the manifesto was a radical document in any way, and it ought to be contrasted with the Conservative manifesto to see if there are any major differences in either ideology or policy. The main target appeared to be the middle-ground voter, who would be alienated by anything that looked too radical or 'socialist'.

The role of the manifesto in Labour's victory needs to be known, and also its possible influence on decreasing voter turnout.

Initial evidence coming from the analysis of the 2001 general election indicates that it achieved its objective. However, one of the reasons for the low turnout of voters — particularly among the social groups that traditionally support Labour (its **core vote**) — is that it contained too little which appealed to the poorer sections of the community, such as radically increased spending on benefits and pensions.

C Leadership selection

The methods of
leadership selection in
the three major parties
need to be known.

SELECTION OF CONSERVATIVE PARTY LEADER

Until 1965 the Conservative method of leadership selection involved discreet consultation among senior members of the party, with the monarch sometimes taking a view as well. It is known that the queen was influential in choosing, for example, Sir Alec Douglas-Home in 1963. The fact that many Conservatives saw him as a particularly incompetent leader led to demands to change a method that many considered inappropriate to a party in a twentieth-century democracy.

This system of leadership selection changed in 1965 to the one that chose William Hague in 1997. Selection was made only by Conservative MPs. No party members or parliamentary candidates were involved, but MPs were expected to consult their local party members. If 10% of Conservative MPs wanted a leadership election, they could have one. There was then a series of ballots until one candidate achieved an overall majority of the votes of all Conservative MPs.

William Hague, selected
by the old method,
tried to make the
Conservative Party a
more 'democratic'
organisation.

William Hague was elected by Conservative MPs in 1997, but he introduced changes that now permit party members to be involved in the final selection, with all members having one vote. Iain Duncan Smith was chosen by this method in 2001.

SELECTION OF LABOUR PARTY LEADER

Before 1983 the Labour Party leader was elected by a ballot process open only to Labour MPs. As part of a series of reforms intended to make the party more democratic after the election defeat of 1979, a system known as an **electoral college** was introduced.

The Labour Party also
adopted a more
'democratic' method of
leadership selection
after a massive electoral
defeat.

In this electoral college system, one-third of the total vote in the college is given to MPs and MEPs (Members of the European Parliament), one-third to members of trade unions that are affiliated to the Labour Party and one-third to ordinary party members. In both the unions and the constituency parties there is **OMOV** (one member, one vote). In the past, trade unions could vote on behalf of their members (known as the **block vote**) and this gave the leaders huge influence over who was elected Labour leader. One trade union leader might be able to cast several hundred thousand votes; now each member of a union has to be balloted separately.

SELECTION OF LIBERAL DEMOCRAT LEADER

The leader has to be an MP and each member of the party is allowed one vote.

D Selection of parliamentary candidates

SELECTION OF CONSERVATIVE PARTY CANDIDATES

Potential candidates usually apply to Conservative Central Office and go through a vetting process operated by the candidate selection officer, who is appointed by the party leader. This gives the party leader a lot of influence. If approved by Central Office, a possible candidate is then put on the 'approved list' of candidates. The approved candidate may apply for any advertised vacancy in a parliamentary constituency.

The local constituency then short-lists the applicants (there can be a large number in a safe Conservative seat) and makes the final choice. There is limited scope for the ordinary party member to be involved in the process, as much of it is conducted by the Executive Council of the local Conservative Association. However, it is normal for members of the local association to select the candidate from the short-listed group after the applicants have spoken to them and answered their questions.

Traditionally, Central Office has exercised only limited control over local associations and has intervened only selectively in local matters. For example, when Michael Portillo lost his seat in the 1997 general election, he had to wait until there was a vacancy (caused by the death of the sitting MP) in the constituency of Kensington and Chelsea, and then apply to the local Conservative Association along with many others for the vacant candidature. It is suggested that there might have been pressure from William Hague and Central Office to get Michael Portillo back into parliament, but in the end the local association is free to choose whom it wishes.

SELECTION OF LABOUR PARTY CANDIDATES

A would-be Labour candidate must first join the party. Although Head Office has an approved list of parliamentary candidates, local parties do not have to choose a candidate from it. Other local groups, such as trade unions, may also put forward candidates. The National Executive Committee (NEC) of the party imposes specific rules about who may be short-listed: for example, there has to be at least one woman on a short-list. Then all local members and members of affiliated unions are allowed one vote each.

However, there is now much less union influence over candidate selection and much more NEC and leadership control than before. Since 1995 the NEC has refused to accept some candidates chosen locally, and has even imposed its own candidates on some constituencies. This is a major change for the Labour Party, which had always allowed much greater local control than the Conservative Party did.

Increasing the ability of the leader and the NEC to decide on suitable candidates has been a major part of the Labour Party's 'modernisation' programme. Neil Kinnock and Tony Blair wanted to stop local constituencies choosing candidates from the radical or 'left' wing of the party, and therefore alienating the middle-ground voter felt to be vital for Labour success in general elections. One of the best examples of this came in 1983, when Peter Tatchell, a prominent gay-rights campaigner who advocated radical social and socialist polices, became the Labour candidate for the constituency of Bermondsey in London. Bermondsey had been a very safe Labour seat, but the press in the election campaign highlighted the 'extremism' of Peter Tatchell and the Liberal Democrats won the seat. They have held it ever since.

Be prepared to comment on how 'democratic' the candidate selection process is.

Again, be prepared to analyse how 'democratic' the selection of candidates is in the Labour Party.

One of the most difficult tasks facing the leadership of a political party — which is, of course, a vital part of the democratic process — is how democratic that party can be itself. Consider what is the most appropriate action for a democratically elected party leader to take when a tiny minority of party members choose parliamentary candidates whom the leader believes will lead to the party losing seats or even the general election.

E The role of party conferences

All the major parties have annual conferences, which take place in the autumn of each year.

LABOUR PARTY CONFERENCE
The Labour conference has several main functions. These are:
- to direct and control the party as a whole — in theory, the conference is the 'sovereign' body within the party
- to give ordinary members a chance to air their views, vote on issues and elect people to key positions in the party, such as membership of the NEC
- to enable ministers or shadow ministers to argue for new policies and test party opinion on them
- to make ministers debate and defend their policies if the party is in government
- to enable communication upwards and downwards within the party
- to allow ordinary members to meet the party's MPs and leaders

Overall the conference has lost power and influence in recent years and the leadership has grown more powerful. In addition, very great care is now taken by the party leadership to control the agenda of conference, as well as those who may speak, so that the party does not debate divisive issues or appear disunited. The media that attend will focus very closely on possible divisions within the party, and the electorate is thought to disapprove of disunited parties at election time.

However, in 1996 (when Labour was in opposition) the conference helped persuade the Labour leadership to include constitutional reform in the party's manifesto; and the 2000 conference (when Labour was in government) was very influential in persuading the chancellor Gordon Brown to improve old age pensions.

CONSERVATIVE PARTY CONFERENCE
Unlike the Labour conference, the Conservative Party conference has no formal role. However, it is seen as important in the following ways:
- to rally party members
- to obtain open endorsement of policies already decided by the leadership
- to test out new ideas
- to enhance the status of ministers or shadow ministers

Look up each party's website and examine the issues raised and debated at its party conference. This will give you a good picture of the key policies advocated by each party.

The Labour conference is decreasing in importance as the power of the party leadership grows. Consider the democratic implications of this.

F

- to give an opportunity for communication between the party's leadership and its ordinary membership
- via the media, to improve the image of the party, to demonstrate unity and support for the leader, and to appeal to voters

Traditionally, conference is not seen as an important part of Conservative Party processes. The leadership might respond to strong pressure sensed at conference, but that is unusual. The Conservative Party is seen as a much more 'top-down' organisation than the supposedly more democratic Labour Party.

The role of party leaders

LABOUR PARTY LEADER

Traditionally, the Labour leader was expected to behave in a more 'democratic' way than his Conservative counterpart, and to be much more obedient to the National Executive Committee, party conference, the trade unions and the parliamentary party. However, as a result of losing four elections in a row — in 1979, 1983, 1987 and 1992 — the party's desire to form a government overcame its traditional 'democratic' tendencies and enabled Neil Kinnock, John Smith and then Tony Blair to change the role of the Labour leader out of all recognition.

The Labour Party leader now pays far less attention to the unions, the NEC and conference. Kinnock and Blair have broken the militant left, abandoned traditional socialist ideas and eliminated many areas of dissent within the party. The leader now has far more control over Labour MPs and local parties. Tony Blair is a far more powerful figure within the party, when it comes to making party policy and selecting parliamentary candidates, than any of his predecessors. He has insisted on far greater discipline within the party, both inside and outside parliament, and has gained it.

Tony Blair has been accused by critics both inside and outside the party of being a 'control freak'. But his defenders argue that the Labour Party would not have won two elections in a row, and achieved as much as it has, between 1997 and 2001 if he had not had a disciplined and united party. Blair now insists on playing a central role in drafting the Labour Party manifesto, and has done so for both the 1997 and 2001 elections. Controlling the manifesto obviously gives the party leader control over the policy agenda of the government if it wins the election.

Tony Blair also imposed his own view of how general elections should be conducted. Labour campaigns are now run from a separate headquarters at Millbank, removed from Labour Party head office. The winning election team of 1997, led by Peter Mandelson, Alastair Campbell and Bryan Gould, reported very much to Blair, and not to the general secretary of the party as had been the case in the past.

CONSERVATIVE PARTY LEADER

In theory, the Conservative leader is much more powerful than the Labour leader:
- The leader is free to choose both the cabinet and shadow cabinet (the Labour Party's shadow cabinet is elected).

At present the Conservative conference has even less influence and power than the Labour conference. It is possible that with the Hague reforms, which give the membership more influence, conference will become more important as a policy-maker.

The role of the Labour leader has changed quite radically since 1983. Again, consider the implications of this for democracy.

- The leader has total control of the election manifesto, which in effect makes party policy.
- The leader appoints the party chairperson (the Labour equivalent is elected by conference); this gives the leader control of the party machine and the initial vetting of parliamentary candidates.
- The leader is not obliged to pay any attention to the wishes of conference, while in the Labour Party the conference is supposed to be 'sovereign'.
- The new constitution of the party actually states that 'the Leader shall determine the political direction of the party'.
- Hierarchy and strong leadership seem to be basic Conservative beliefs.

Traditionally, a Conservative leader found it easier to impose his or her personality and ideas on the party than a Labour leader.

> It is possible that William Hague may have made the Conservative Party more 'democratic', but commentators feel it is unlikely to happen in the near future.

G Funding of political parties

The way in which political parties obtain the money needed to function has become a major issue in recent years. In the past, business funded the Conservative Party and the trade unions funded the Labour Party. Both parties were regularly criticised for being too dependent on a single source for their funding, and therefore likely to be too influenced when in government by the source of their funds. Labour governments were accused of favouring the 'working class' as the bulk of their funds came from the large public sector trade unions, such as the Post Office workers. The Conservative Party was criticised for being too 'boss' orientated, as it gained the bulk of its funding from major companies, such as the Commercial Union Insurance Company. Usually only a very small percentage of party income came from the membership, and in both major parties membership has been falling rapidly in recent decades.

There is a growing expectation from the public of better performance by political parties, but parties face a decline in their income. As both unions and business are unhappy about the 'return' they have been getting on their investment, they are giving less money to the parties.

> There is now a high level of criticism about how parties are funded.

In the general election of 1997, the Conservatives spent £28 million, Labour £26 million and the Liberals £2 million, leading inevitably to the accusation that money can 'buy' elections. It was also felt to be very unfair on the Liberal Democrats that they could not compete with the two major parties, as they were unable to raise their profile without greater funding. They argued strongly that lack of funding deprived the electorate of a real 'choice'.

REFORM OF THE FUNDING OF POLITICAL PARTIES

Several funding scandals that affected both parties ('Cash for Questions' and the Ecclestone affair) led to Tony Blair's government asking the Neill Committee on Standards in Public Life (initially set up by John Major) to look at the whole issue of the funding of political parties. The Neill Report recommended:

> Look at the Ashcroft and Hinduja affairs.

- no foreign donations — both major parties had been criticised for taking money from people abroad

- public knowledge of all large donations, so that at least the public would know who was funding parties
- a £20 million cap on spending by a party at general elections — this would ease the money-raising problems of the two major parties, but give little comfort to the Liberal Democrats and other small parties
- an increase in state funding, particularly for opposition parties
- that shareholders should approve company donations to a political party, in the same way that union members have to approve union donations to a political party
- fair funding for both 'sides' in referendums — it was felt that the government of the day was able to influence referendum results too easily

Although the report led to clear limits on election spending for the Scottish Parliament and Welsh Assembly elections in 1998, nothing has happened to implement these recommendations in other respects, and they did not apply to the election of 2001.

THE FUNDING OF THE 2001 GENERAL ELECTION

Precise figures are not yet available, but it is known that the Labour Party spent nearly its permitted figure of £14 million on its 'central office' campaign. This is different from what local parties may spend, which is very tightly regulated. The Labour Party did not find it easy to raise this money as trade unions such as the GMB have reduced their support in protest at some New Labour policies. In addition, membership is down from over 400,000 in 1997 to about 280,000 in summer 2001, which has reduced income severely.

The Labour Party is now increasingly dependent on donations from rich businessmen such as Lord Sainsbury and the late Lord Hamlyn, and is suffering from the sorts of criticism that Labour itself directed at the Conservatives in previous years. Because of a shortage of cash, the Labour Party is closing its Millbank office and making party workers redundant.

The Conservative Party, under the treasurership of the controversial foreign-based billionaire Lord Ashcroft (made a peer by a grateful Conservative Party!), is in a much better financial state. Its Central Office election bill for the 2001 general election was £9.3 million. Conservative Party finances are seen as very healthy. It has paid all its debts for the election and is in surplus. It was helped by two £5 million donations from individual businessmen, but Lord Ashcroft has also substantially increased the number of members who have agreed to pay at least £10,000 a year.

In addition to the funds that the two major parties spend on a general election centrally — on making party political broadcasts, national advertising and leaders touring the country — parties are allowed to spend locally. For the 2001 election, every party was allowed to spend £5,483 and 6.2p per elector in a rural constituency and slightly less in an urban one.

STATE FUNDING OF PARTIES

The following arguments are made in favour of state funding of parties:
- It would remove the large sums that the two parties get from private donors, who might have sinister and selfish objectives in giving a party money.

● It would help the minority parties and eliminate the criticism that elections can be 'bought'.

● Parties perform such a vital role in a democracy that they really ought to be fairly and ethically funded.

● Many feel that the opposition is unable to do its work properly as it lacks the funding to research policy and provide an effective alternative to the government of the day.

● The leader of the opposition is paid, as is the opposition chief whip, and there is a small contribution towards running the leader of the opposition's office. However, the opposition shadow cabinet gets no assistance from the state in its work.

At present Tony Blair has rejected the idea of state funding of parties, although the principal opposition party does get some state funding.

There are, however, a number of arguments against the idea of state funding:

● How much a party should get would be difficult to work out.

● Many people might dislike the idea of their hard-earned tax money going to radical or extremist parties.

● The UK is a free society, and individuals who wish to give a large (or small) sum of money to a party should be free to do so.

H Declining party membership

The Conservative Party's membership declined from 2.8 million in the 1950s to around 300,000 in 1997, whilst the Labour Party's membership fell from 1 million to 400,000 over the same period. The key reasons for the decline in party membership are as follows:

● Young people now tend to participate in the political process in different ways, such as protest politics and pressure groups.

● All ages have found it easier to achieve objectives by pressure group membership.

Find out more about these examples of alleged 'sleaze'.

● Politicians have not had a good image recently. Recent examples are the Mandelson, Robinson and Hinduja affairs with Labour, and the Hamilton and Ashcroft affairs with the Conservatives.

● The move of some decision making to Brussels has given the impression that less can be achieved by participating in local or national politics.

● It is no longer necessary to join a political party in order to get political information.

Decreasing party membership is matched by a decreasing turnout in all elections — especially the 2001 election.

● There is an increased perception that membership of a political party will not achieve anything.

I The role of political parties

Political parties provide several vital functions in the British democratic process. This is surprising considering that they are not popular organisations and they now attract few members and limited finance.

The most important functions of political parties are:

● to provide the government and the opposition parties in parliament

- to enable the government of the day to get its legislation passed by parliament
- to recruit, train and promote politicians
- to offer voters a choice at election time, at national, local and European level
- to enable individuals to participate effectively in the political process — and to influence the decisions that affect their lives
- to enable the views of the public to be represented in parliament or councils
- to link the government in London or Edinburgh with the individual in the localities
- to enable popular wishes to be transformed into policy or law

In summary, political parties are the means by which politics can be made to work in a democratic society. Without parties, mass democracy would be unworkable, as there is no way in which every individual can participate directly in all the decision-making processes of a democratic society.

Consider very carefully the critical role of political parties in the democratic process.

J Key terms and concepts

Adversarial politics Once referred to as a 'stand-up fight between the two main political parties for the benefit of the lookers on'. It is a system where there is always one party in government and one in opposition committed to criticising the government. Some argue that this leads to negative and damaging politics and that there should be more focus on 'consensus politics', where parties aim to reach broad agreement.

Consensus Broad agreement within a group. For example, there was broad agreement (consensus) among all political parties in the 1950s and 1960s that the National Health Service should remain and be fully funded.

Conservatism An ideology that aims to keep what is best in society and opposes radical change. It can be a more flexible ideology (and more difficult to define) than either liberalism or socialism, as Conservatives can embrace radical change, such as entry into the EU.

Democracy Originally a system of government where all qualified citizens participated directly in the decision-making process. The term is now used to describe a system where the citizen chooses a representative from competing political parties — hence the vital importance of parties to the democratic process.

Ideology A thorough and consistent set of ideas by which a group of people can make sense of the world of politics. It is a broad set of ideas that may offer an explanation of how present politics have arisen, an indication of where politics might be going and a broad plan of action based on known ideas. It is not to be confused with 'policy', although policies may be based on ideology. It could be argued that the current Labour ideology is the 'Third Way', between the ideologies of capitalism and socialism, and the policies of the 'Third Way' are laid down in the Labour manifesto of 2001.

Liberalism A political ideology that has as its main beliefs the preservation of the rights of the individual and giving all citizens the maximum freedom of choice. It focuses on the liberty of the individual and sees the purpose of the state as being to help the individual.

Manifestos and mandates A party manifesto is a list of policies that a political party promises to carry out if it wins the election, such as cutting taxation.

All major parties publish a manifesto during an election campaign. A mandate (simply 'permission') is what a party has when it wins an election and forms a government. It then feels that it has been given permission (a mandate) by the electorate to carry out the policies in its manifesto.

Policy A specific plan. One of the main policies laid down in the Labour Party manifesto of 2001 was to recruit 20,000 extra nurses into the National Health Service.

Political participation Literally, taking part in politics. By joining a political party a citizen can take part, or participate, in the decision-making process, choosing candidates and leaders and being involved in the making of party policy.

Representation The relationship between a group and the person chosen (usually by a political party) to protect and promote the interests of that group. Again make sure that the differences between a representative (a free agent) and a delegate (one bound by instructions) are clearly known.

Socialism A political (and economic) ideology based on the state or the community owning the main means of production (e.g. steel factories), distribution (transport) and exchange (banks, etc). The welfare of the individual is less important than the welfare of the community as a whole. A socialist would see equality as a more important goal than individual freedom.

This topic is central to the study of Government and Politics. Be careful when using out-of-date textbooks, as they do not give the topic the priority it now warrants. Two of the three examination boards (OCR and AQA) devote a whole unit to pressure groups, while the topic clearly forms a major part of Edexcel's Unit 1. It is vital not only to have a good academic knowledge of the work of pressure groups, but also to have plenty of recent examples of their work and their growing influence in the whole political process.

One of the best ways of studying pressure groups is to log on to various pressure group websites and see exactly what they do. Good examples are the Countryside Alliance, Liberty, the Terence Higgins Trust and PROP.

Key questions

What are the main different types of pressure group?

How do pressure groups attain their objectives?

Why are some pressure groups successful?

What harm or benefits do pressure groups bring to the democratic process?

What has been the impact of membership of the EU on UK pressure groups?

How important are pressure groups?

A What is a pressure group?

DEFINITION

A pressure group is an organised group of people who do not stand for election to parliament, local government, etc. but who hope to influence the government or other decision-makers. A small group of householders getting together to stop the local council putting an approved school near their homes is a pressure group, as is the Campaign for Nuclear Disarmament (CND), which seeks to change the UK into a non-nuclear country.

Basic definitions are frequently asked for.

PRESSURE GROUPS AND POLITICAL PARTIES

It is important to understand the key differences between a pressure group and a political party. A political party actively seeks to become the government, and not just to influence it. A political party may want to appeal to many different pressure groups in order to win an election. A political party that seeks to appeal to just one interest group, such as business or trade unions, risks losing an election by having too limited an appeal.

B Types of pressure group

Political scientists tend to use different words to classify the many different types of pressure group. Indeed, they often use the term 'interest group' instead of pressure group. Words like 'promotional', 'peak', 'episodic' and 'attitude cause'

Both the specimen
papers and the first set
of AS-level papers asked
for definitions and
examples of different
types of pressure group.

are sometimes used. The best advice is just to learn the four main groups listed below, as these are universally accepted, particularly by examiners.

INSIDER GROUPS

These are pressure groups that the government considers respectable and well informed, and with which it likes to be associated. Insider groups are usually given direct and frequent access to ministers and government departments, and when a government is drafting a policy or a new law, an insider group would expect to be consulted by the government and have its views taken very seriously. Good examples of insider groups are the National Farmers' Union (NFU) and the British Medical Association (BMA). The government worked very closely with the NFU in order to develop a policy to deal with the foot-and-mouth crisis of 2001.

There can be risks attached to the government allowing too much 'insider' status to a pressure group. Some argue that because the relationship is so close between, for example, the government and the NFU, the public interest suffers. Examples of the possible damage done by insider groups are the role of the NFU in the BSE crisis and the role of the BMA in the Bristol heart surgery cases.

Ensure that you know
several examples of
insider groups, as well
as the merits and
demerits of such groups.

Very often insider groups are given legal powers by the government to regulate their members, such as the power of the BMA to ban doctors from practising medicine. They often help the government to draft laws or make policy, as they have a lot of expert knowledge.

OUTSIDER GROUPS

These are groups that do not wish to be closely associated with government, or are unable to gain any formal recognition from government. Examples are the Campaign for Nuclear Disarmament (CND) and the Countryside Alliance. The government would not dream of consulting CND on defence policy, although it is aware of CND's viewpoint.

Again, ensure you know
recent examples. A brief
study of the whole
foxhunting issue will
give you a huge range
of excellent examples of
pressure group politics.

Some outsider groups, such as the Countryside Alliance, might like to become 'insider' groups. Part of the Countryside Alliance's campaign was against the 'insider' status given to the NFU, which it felt had too much influence over the government and did not adequately represent those who lived in the countryside. The huge turnout of peaceful demonstrators that the Countryside Alliance achieved in London in 1999 (over 200,000 people) is a good example of the effectiveness of this type of pressure group politics. It evidently made the Labour government of the day rethink its policy on foxhunting.

SECTIONAL GROUPS

These represent a particular section of society, such as motor manufacturers, teachers, lawyers or patients. They aim to look after the interests of that particular group and either to stop things happening which they feel might harm that group (e.g. taking away patients' right to see their medical records) or to make things happen which will benefit that group (e.g. lowering the retirement age for teachers).

Find examples of
successful sectional
group activity.

There are many recent examples of sectional group activity. The trade unions representing railway workers have resisted the policy to privatise the London

Underground, while the Postal Workers' Union is also resisting attempts to privatise the mail delivery system. On the other hand, the pressure group that represents the owners of small rural post offices works exceptionally hard to try and ensure that there is further privatisation of postal services, as it feels that this is very much in the interest of its members. One of the advantages of pressure group politics in this case is that the government, the media and the public are made aware of the differing sides of this complex argument.

CAUSE GROUPS

There are two main types of cause group. One is a group set up to achieve a single limited objective, such as to stop a motorway going through a particular site. The other has a broader, longer-term objective, such as the Child Poverty Action Group, which campaigns to end child poverty. This objective may not only take time to achieve, but also require many different methods to be used.

Shelter, a pressure group that deals with homelessness, provides an excellent example of a cause group and might be useful in dealing with almost any question on pressure groups. The media had a huge impact on the creation of Shelter — particularly a TV drama/documentary called *Cathy Come Home*, which was widely reported in the press and followed up by detailed newspaper reports on homelessness and the plight of those living on the streets. Shelter was set up in the wake of this increase in awareness, and benefited from the excellent leadership of Des Wilson (now seen as an expert on pressure group politics). The group was then able to raise substantial funds, which it used not only to provide shelter for the homeless, but also to put pressure on parliament, the relevant government departments and, above all, local government to ensure that more was done to provide for the homeless. Wilson and Shelter succeeded in keeping pressure on the right people and backed this up by clever use of the media in order to maintain public sympathy and awareness. Thus Shelter is a good example of how pressure group politics can benefit the democratic process.

Two more recent examples also warrant consideration:
- The Snowdrop Campaign followed the appalling massacre of children and their teacher by a gunman at a school in Dunblane. This pressure group, formed largely by parents of the young victims, but backed by huge media support and widespread public sympathy, rapidly achieved the passage of a law to ban all handguns in the UK. In this sense it is an example of a highly successful pressure group. However, a more critical view might be that 'gun crime' has continued to rise, and that the rights and interests of responsible gun owners and their clubs were not 'democratically' considered. Is this an example of a minority imposing their views on a majority?
- A number of babies died, or suffered unnecessarily, as a result of flawed surgery by a group of paediatric (child) heart surgeons in Bristol during the 1990s. It is worth looking into the campaign organised by the babies' parents — the way in which they got together, organised themselves, raised limited funds, gained some media support and tried to find out what had actually happened to their babies, and why. They succeeded in getting certain surgeons 'struck' off or disciplined, and received an admission from the hospital concerned that what had happened to their babies was wrong and would not

Make sure that examples of the impact of cause groups on government are known.

be repeated in future on other babies. The government instituted a major public inquiry, and when it reported in July 2001 it made headline news in all the newspapers and dominated radio and television news. It has led to major changes in hospital procedures and their monitoring. If the evidence presented to the inquiry is looked at in detail, there are many other examples of pressure group activity there. The paediatric heart surgeons were represented by 'their' pressure group, as were the criticised hospital administrators.

C The role of pressure groups

ressure groups perform a vital role in our democratic process. If we did not tolerate pressure groups, we could not call ourselves a democracy.

The positive role of pressure groups is a standard AS question — learn your response.

POSITIVE FUNCTIONS

- They enable individuals to participate in the national political process between elections. For example, you can join a group to ban foxhunting even though you might have voted for an MP or party that favours it. Pressure groups give ✓citizens another voice in the decision-making process.
- They are a useful way for individuals to participate in local politics, besides voting. Pressure groups are formed to try and persuade a council to keep open a village school, for example, or to try and persuade the local planning committee to refuse permission for a branch of McDonald's to open in an ✓ area.
- They ensure that minorities, such as homosexuals, AIDS sufferers or those who wish to close all shops on Sundays, can make their voice heard. They help to prevent a 'tyranny of the majority', where the majority impose possibly ✓ intolerant policies on a minority group in the community.
- They make the government aware of views other than those coming through the political parties or the civil service. For example, the 'official' view is that genetically modified crops, widely grown in the USA, are perfectly safe. However, certain pressure groups in the UK have hindered their development (sometimes using illegal methods) and insisted that there is further debate on the issue. Whether it is 'democratic' for such a minority to hold back what ✓ other people might see as real progress is important to debate.
- They can bring expert knowledge to the government's attention on an important issue. An example is the Royal Society for the Prevention of Accidents (RoSPA), whose membership includes many very experienced casualty doctors. They helped the movement draw up the legislation required to make seatbelts ✓ compulsory.
- They can generate new ideas that practising politicians often do not have time to consider. This type of pressure group is sometimes known as a 'think-tank'. ✓ Some had a major influence on Margaret Thatcher and her economic policies.
- They are a way in which groups that are not seen as electorally important, ✓ such as students, can make their views known.

THE DANGERS OF PRESSURE GROUPS

There are several ways in which pressure groups can harm the democratic process:

- They can be sectional and selfish. One powerful group can dominate an issue, such as health care. The GPs and consultants are very powerfully organised, and nurses and patients may lose out as a result.
- They can be so skilled at putting pressure on ministers and parliament that the latter forget the general public. For example, in the cases of salmonella in eggs and BSE in cows, it is argued that the health interests of the general public were not the primary concern of ministers and civil servants, but that not upsetting the NFU and farmers was seen as more important.
- A few elite groups dominate society — as one writer put it, 'in pluralist heaven the heavenly choir sings with a strong upper class accent'. The Bar Council, which looks after the interests of barristers, is a good example here. Many critics of the legal system, with its high costs and slowness, and the need to employ both a solicitor and a barrister in major cases, feel that the Bar Council's dominant position is a barrier to reform. The large number of lawyers in politics (including Tony Blair and his wife) is sometimes felt to prevent law reforms that would be in the public interest.
- Pressure groups are very good at stopping things happening which other people may feel are actually needed. When the building of the M42 was held up by pressure groups for 14 years, Midlands industry and employment were estimated to have suffered considerably as a result. Animal rights groups came close to shutting down the Huntingdon Life Sciences firm, which tested drugs on animals prior to their use on humans. Drugs firms (through their own pressure groups) argued that major health benefits to humans would be blocked if their products were not tested on animals, and that jobs and wealth would be lost in the UK if the firm closed and the work were carried out abroad.
- They can cause social disharmony, as those groups that are not well organised lose out to those that are. Consider the conflict between the Lord's Day Observance Society and the supermarkets over Sunday trading. Shops that wished to open on Sunday organised themselves into a very powerful pressure group, and raised a lot of money to pressurise parliament to change the law. The Lord's Day Observance Society simply could not match their resources, although polls at the time indicated a fair amount of popular support for their cause. The retail trade unions, who opposed Sunday opening on behalf of their members, also could not match the resources of the supermarkets. The majority of those union members opposed the change.
- Small numbers of people who are not elected or really representative of the membership dominate some groups. The non-elected leadership of one of the motoring organisations, for example, opposed the compulsory wearing of seat belts, but a newspaper poll of the organisation's members revealed overwhelming support for the measure. Be aware of the 'undemocratic' structure of some pressure groups.

Look at the methods used by some of the animal rights campaigners to stop the Huntingdon employees doing their work, and efforts made to prevent others, such as banks, from having any dealings with them.

A standard question on pressure groups concerns the possible harm they might do to the democratic process.

D Pressure group methods

Pressure groups tend to use different methods at different times to achieve their objectives. The normal range of methods used is listed below.

- **Seeking to influence the government directly.** Pressure groups may try to get access to the key decision-makers — the prime minister, cabinet ministers and civil servants — and argue their case directly.

- **Seeking to influence MPs.** They may try to influence MPs either individually or collectively, or target members of specific standing or select committees or parties. A good example is when Charter 88, a pressure group wanting major constitutional reform, targeted Labour MPs, candidates and party members in 1996–97 to get constitutional reform into the 1997 Labour manifesto. Another is when David Steel's Abortion Bill, legalising abortion, went through the committee stage in the House of Commons — pressure groups ensured it was amended so that Roman Catholic nurses and doctors were not compelled to undertake tasks they found morally repugnant.

- **Seeking to influence members of the House of Lords.** This is particularly likely when the Lords is debating or revising bills that have come up from the Commons. The many financial benefits that organisations dealing with the housing of the elderly get are mainly due to an alliance of pressure groups (e.g. Help the Aged) persuading members of the House of Lords to make certain amendments to the Housing Finance Act, and then persuading the House of Commons to accept those amendments.

- **Seeking to influence key local officials.** These include planning officers and local councillors. With the usual low turnout in local elections, local councillors tend to be very responsive to local issues.

- **Launching a major media campaign.** Examples are the Snowdrop Campaign over the Dunblane massacre and the effect of the mass media on the fuel price protest in autumn 2000.

- **Advertising.** There is considerable disagreement about how effective advertising might be, but major groups such as Greenpeace and animal rights groups use it extensively at times. ASH, the anti-smoking pressure group, is another group that uses advertising extensively. An interesting exercise is to consider why ASH could be seen as an unsuccessful pressure group.

- **Hiring professional lobbyists.** These lobbyists specialise in influencing government. It is accepted that one of the reasons why the £5 billion contract to maintain the UK's nuclear submarines went to Devonport and not Rosyth in Scotland was because of the millions that Devonport spent in hiring a company that specialises in pressurising government (and has quite a lot of MPs on its payroll as 'consultants').

- **Legal methods of protest.** These methods include marches and demonstrations, such as the Countryside Alliance demonstration in London, and more forceful tactics, such as strikes and boycotts. There have been far fewer of the latter in recent years.

- **Illegal activities.** Some pressure groups, such as several of the animal rights groups, use violence, civil disobedience and other illegal activities to further their cause.

E Reasons for pressure group success

This is one of the most difficult questions to answer. The Snowdrop Campaign to ban handguns in the UK probably succeeded simply because so many children were killed. There was such a feeling of revulsion nationally that no politician dared stand in the way of the ban on handguns, or listen to the views of the pro-gun pressure group that wanted to keep handguns for clubs. Another great success for pressure politics was when the government awarded the multibillion-pound contract for the repair and servicing of the Trident missile submarines to Devonport, and not to Rosyth in Scotland, because Devonport hired the best lobbyists and paid double the money to win the contract.

Reasons to consider are as follows:
- the support of the media, particularly if it is sustained over a period of time
- the sympathy the government feels for the issue and how many votes it feels it might win or lose — the nearness of an election may well be a factor here
- whether decision-makers are in broad agreement with the pressure group
- the size and possible electoral impact of the membership of the pressure group
- how united the pressure group is (e.g. teachers have at least six different unions that frequently disagree, whereas GPs have one — the BMA — and so the latter is much more likely to be listened to)
- whether it has the resources to employ able managers, to advertise, etc.
- the quality of its organisation and leadership
- the attitude of the public towards the issue (e.g. an environmental disaster will help environmental groups)

Success depends on many different factors, some of which a pressure group has no control over.

F The growth and spread of pressure politics

GROWTH OF PRESSURE GROUP ACTIVITY
There has been a decrease in membership of political parties and a major growth of pressure group activity. Recent examples to consider are:
- the conflict between ASH (the anti-smoking pressure group), backed by the BMA, and the Formula One group over tobacco advertising
- the growth of the Countryside Alliance and the rural lobby
- the attempts to ban foxhunting
- the attempts by pensioners to raise pensions
- the fuel tax protests

Find out who won and why.

Skim back through copies of, for example, *The Economist* to get examples of recent pressure group politics.

PRESSURE GROUPS AND THE EUROPEAN UNION
Now that major decisions in certain areas, such as agriculture and transport, are made in Brussels by the EU, many pressure groups in the UK have either moved

The Confederation of British Industry is the manufacturers' pressure group.

The EU has a very different attitude towards pressure groups from the British government.

to Brussels or set up offices there. Pressure groups such as the National Farmers' Union and the CBI have learned that if they want to influence a proposal (e.g. to change lamb quotas or reduce exhaust emissions), they need to target:

- the European Commission, which draws up the proposal
- the Council of Ministers, which agrees to it
- the European Parliament, which can debate the issue and question the commission
- the European Court of Justice — if need be

The evidence is that when drawing up a proposal that may have an impact on all EU members, the commission is much more open to persuasion from pressure groups than is the UK government.

G Key terms and concepts

Democracy A system of government based on the participation of all qualified citizens in the decision-making processes. Pressure groups are vital for the democratic process, as they are the means through which citizens can participate — in addition to just voting.

Influence The ability to affect decisions through persuasion.

Participation Literally, taking part in politics. Direct political participation might involve joining a party, voting or standing for election. Pressure groups provide a means of indirect participation in politics. A citizen might join a pressure group to stop a motorway, and it will be the organised group that will link with the political processes.

Pluralism Literally, holding more than one idea or doing more than one thing. Pressure groups encourage pluralism, diversity and representation in a democratic society, as a citizen can vote Labour, for instance, but also join a pressure group that campaigns to keep foxhunting.

Pressure The application by groups or individuals of organised persuasion with the intention of affecting decision making.

Representation To act on behalf of, in the way a lawyer 'represents' a client in court. It is the relationship between an individual or group and the person chosen to protect and promote their interests, such as an MP or MSP (Member of the Scottish Parliament). The individual or group, or in this case the constituents, have given the MP/MSP the authority to act on their behalf through the election process.

This topic appears in the specified content of all three examination boards.

OCR has a compulsory question on it in Unit 3, but it is fairly predictable and focuses on the relationship between the UK and the European Union (EU). It is essential to know the key treaties and the way in which they change the relationship between the EU and the UK.

With Edexcel the focus is more on the impact of EU membership on the UK — the issue of sovereignty.

With AQA the subject can appear in either Module 2 or Module 3. In Module 2 the working of British political parties at the European level needs to be known, and also the way in which pressure groups need to focus on the EU in certain areas. For Module 3 there needs to be a good working knowledge of the 'main characteristics' of the European Parliament and the Council of Ministers, and the role of the European Commission in the policy-making process.

There is also a requirement to ensure that the differing positions of the major parties on the EU are known. Candidates need to know what the EU can and cannot do, and what the impact of membership has been on the UK. Make sure that you know and can use correctly all the jargon, such as 'federalism'.

It is vital that you stay up to date on this topic, as it changes constantly. The best way of doing this is by looking regularly at the excellent official EU website, which manages to cover changes in a refreshingly non-partisan way. It is also a good idea to look at the websites of the Labour and Conservative Parties to monitor their views on both the EU and the euro.

Key questions

What is the relationship between the UK and the EU?

What has been the impact of membership of the EU on the UK?

How do the main political parties in the UK differ on the subject of the EU?

What are the main political and constitutional implications for the UK of membership of the EU?

A The European Union and British involvement

IDEAS UNDERLYING THE EU

There have been many attempts to unify Europe in the past, but the main drive towards the present EU came just after the Second World War, mainly from Europeans who wished to have no more wars in Europe. The UK was asked to be a part of what was originally known as the European Economic Community (EEC) when it was set up between 1955 and 1958, but it declined. The British government realised almost immediately, however, that its failure to be involved had been a fundamental error.

The European Economic Community was renamed the European Community (EC) in 1989 and then became the European Union (EU) after the ratification of the Maastricht Treaty in 1993.

Note very carefully the motives for the initial creation of the EEC.

The main principles of the founders of the EEC were:
- to avoid war
- to develop democracy within Europe
- to improve the living standards of all citizens living within the community

These principles are frequently forgotten, but they have been fulfilled.

In order to achieve these main objectives, the six member states (France, Italy, Germany, Belgium, Holland and Luxembourg) aimed:
- to bring the peoples of Europe closer together
- to abolish trade barriers and customs duties between member states
- to create a **tariff barrier** (duties on imports) around the EEC
- to introduce free movement of people, goods and services within the EEC
- to negotiate trade deals, as one unit, with other economic superpowers such as the USA and Japan

The EEC rapidly proved to be of very considerable benefit to its members, and the economies of all six founder members improved. The British economy went into sharp decline at the same time.

The UK's entry process was long and complex, and it divided both main political parties.

THE UK'S ENTRY INTO THE EEC

In 1963 and 1967 the UK tried to join the EEC, first under the Conservatives and then under Labour, but the French refused. The UK finally joined the EEC in 1973, along with Ireland and Denmark. It was Conservative prime minister Edward Heath who pushed the necessary act of parliament through in 1972. Joining the EEC had been part of the Conservatives' election manifesto in 1970, and they had narrowly won the election. Heath therefore felt he had a **mandate** (the permission of the electorate) to take the UK into the EU. There was no national referendum on whether or not the UK should join.

Key members of both major British political parties were opposed to entry, as they disliked the loss of sovereignty and economic independence. Many on the left saw the EEC as a 'rich man's club' and too capitalistic. There was still much debate about membership after the UK had joined, so in 1975 to settle the question the Labour prime minister, Harold Wilson, held a referendum. Just over two-thirds of those who voted wished to remain in the EEC. It is argued that Wilson would not have had the referendum if he had thought that he might lose, and there were also concerns that the question on the ballot paper was worded in a way that encouraged people to vote to stay in. It was not a binding referendum in any case!

Conservative enthusiasm for the EU started to decline under Margaret Thatcher.

THE UK AND THE EEC UNDER THATCHER, 1979-90

Like other more right-wing Conservatives, Margaret Thatcher had been unhappy with EEC entry as it meant that key decisions in areas such as international trade were made by all the member states in Brussels. She was also unhappy with the UK's cash contribution to EEC funds, particularly to support the highly inefficient farming systems in Germany, France and Italy. The Conservatives were growing increasingly reluctant to accept the fact that membership meant that more and more decisions on key economic issues were being taken in Brussels.

Margaret Thatcher was able to reduce the size of the UK's cash contribution, but may also have given the other members the impression that the UK was unhappy with its membership. During her premiership, the Single European Act of 1986 was passed (see below), with surprisingly little debate or controversy given the Conservative Party's later hostility to the EU's development. The last two years of Thatcher's premiership were increasingly dominated by her dislike of certain aspects of Community membership and the direction in which it was going — and the fact that many of her ministers were much more pro-European than she was.

THE UK AND EUROPE UNDER MAJOR, 1990–97

Under John Major the EU became an important and very divisive issue within the Conservative Party.

The issue of Europe dominated the premiership of John Major, especially the period after he won the election of 1992. With a tiny overall majority in the House of Commons, he had many difficulties with some of his backbench MPs; they opposed the further integration into the European Union brought about by the Maastricht Treaty of 1992 (see page 96). The constant divisions within the Conservative Party over Europe played a significant part in the defeat of the Conservatives in the general election of 1997. The government and its European policy were also damaged when circumstances forced it to withdraw from the exchange rate mechanism in 1992, which was followed by huge increases in interest rates.

THE UK AND THE EU UNDER BLAIR, 1997–2001

Initially, Tony Blair was projected as a much stronger European than his Conservative predecessor was. He implemented the Social Chapter, which had been agreed by the EC in 1989, but which Major had declined to implement. This gave workers many fundamental rights, such as a minimum wage and maximum working hours, and Major had refused to implement it on the grounds of costs to employers. Blair has also tried to play a stronger role within the EU and project himself as more European than previous prime ministers.

However, Blair's government chose not to join the single European currency (euro) when it was introduced, and did not commit itself to joining until specific economic criteria had been met. Even then there would be a referendum first, as the Danes had in 2000. The Labour manifesto of 2001 was cautious on the euro, and it was noted that in his cabinet reshuffle after the 2001 election, Blair removed some of the stronger supporters of the euro from key positions in the decision-making process (e.g. Robin Cook was removed as foreign secretary) and replaced them by politicians less sympathetic to the euro. At the time of writing — August 2001 — the likelihood of the UK joining the euro does not seem strong.

B Key European treaties

THE SINGLE EUROPEAN ACT, 1986

The main provisions of this act, which was agreed to by all of the existing members, including the UK, were as follows:
- to increase the number of member states to 12

- to develop the exchange rate mechanism of the European Monetary Union (the UK did not join until 1990)
- to increase the scope of EEC control in areas such as the environment, research and technology. This gave more power and influence to the European Commission, in particular
- to develop a completely free internal market for goods, labour and capital by 1992. This considerably decreased the ability of member governments to control these factors in their own states
- to increase the role and potential of the European Parliament. This decreased the role of individual national parliaments. However, the citizens of the UK would elect Members of the European Parliament (MEPs)
- to change the voting system within the EEC to prevent a single nation stopping any major change. This ended the **veto** that any one state might have over legislation. It meant that the majority of European states could impose their will on a single state — in other words, citizens of the UK might have to accept a law (e.g. on car exhaust emissions) that their own government had opposed

It is worth stressing that this act was agreed to by Margaret Thatcher and passed by a Conservative-dominated House of Commons with limited debate. Given later opposition by the Conservatives to the EU, this is very surprising.

THE MAASTRICHT TREATY, 1992

Many argue that the meeting that led to the signing of the Maastricht Treaty was the most important meeting of European Community prime ministers since the EEC was set up in the 1950s. The main provisions were:

- agreement to work towards 'ever closer union'
- changing the organisation's name from the European Community to the European Union
- extending the EU's competence into areas such as immigration and foreign policy
- further altering the voting system to stop individual nations holding up the wishes of the majority
- aiming to achieve monetary union, with a single European currency and a central European bank (the UK opted out of this provision)
- recognition of the principle of **subsidiarity** (where decisions are taken at the lowest possible level)
- further enlargement of the EU
- extending the power of the European Parliament

John Major got this treaty through the House of Commons only after a lot of difficulty with his own party and the cabinet.

There was no specific mention of **federalism** in the treaty, mainly because the British government would not have it. However, it is argued that Maastricht was a step towards a federal Europe (see page 98).

THE AMSTERDAM TREATY, 1997

Accepting this treaty was one of Tony Blair's first actions as prime minister. It is argued that the treaty relaxed the drive towards greater centralisation of power in Brussels that had been seen in the Single European Act and the Maastricht Treaty. There had been strong opposition to Maastricht in many other European countries besides the UK. The main results of the Amsterdam Treaty were as follows:

In some respects, Labour can be seen as more enthusiastic 'Europeans' than the Conservatives, but clearly Labour has some reservations.

- The UK accepted the Social Chapter.
- The European Parliament was strengthened.
- Key moves were made towards the single currency (the UK opted out again).

- Human rights legislation, especially in areas such as freedom from discrimination, was tightened.
- The UK was allowed to keep its border controls, but free movement of people was extended elsewhere.

Many 'pro-Europeans' were disappointed by the lack of progress in giving more power to the main European institutions, such as the European Parliament, and by the failure to reform major parts of the EU, such as the Common Agricultural Policy.

THE NICE TREATY, 2000

The main terms of the Nice Treaty were drafted by the European Commission and agreed by the intergovernmental conference that met in Nice in February 2000. It completed its discussions in December 2000 and the treaty was signed in 2001. An intergovernmental conference is where the 15 heads of government of all the member states (e.g. the British prime minister) meet to make major changes in the structure or nature of the EU. These changes have to be agreed by either the parliaments of the 15 member states or a referendum in those countries. The main changes agreed were as follows:

- Progress should be made towards enlarging the EU to include a further 12 countries. Most of these are in eastern Europe, such as Bulgaria and Poland, but they also include countries like Malta and Cyprus.
- The European Parliament should develop into a co-legislator alongside the European Commission, thereby having a greater role in drawing up European legislation. The treaty also worked out how the European Parliament should be organised when enlargement came about.
- The decision-making process within the Council — the top decision-maker in the EU — was changed. With a possible 30 members it would be very difficult to get unanimous decisions when voting took place, so only a two-thirds majority would be needed, except in areas that changed the EU fundamentally. The two-thirds majority did not mean two-thirds of the members of the Council, but members who represented two-thirds of the people of the EU.
- With enlargement there would now be one commissioner per country, and the larger countries, such as the UK, which had two commissioners in the past, would be reduced to one.
- There would be reform of the way in which the Court of Justice operated, as it was getting too overloaded with cases.
- There would also be reform of the Court of Auditors, which is responsible for checking the EU accounts. This was done largely because of complaints about waste and inefficiency in the EU. The vice-president of the EU, the former Labour leader Neil Kinnock, has been given a particular responsibility to reform the EU accounting and monitoring process.
- The process by which the democratic values of the EU are maintained was improved, and more 'teeth' were given to the EU to insist on them.

In addition, an agenda was set for the EU to consider and decide on at the next intergovernmental conference in 2004. The main points were:

- simplifying all the EU treaties into one document
- clarifying the roles of all parts of the EU, such as the commission, and making it clear how they relate to the executives of the member states

As the AS specifications were largely drafted in 1998–99, many will not refer to the Nice Treaty.

- clarifying the Charter of Fundamental Rights
- clarifying the role of the national parliaments within the EU

Overall the Nice Treaty carried on the process of integration that started with the Single European Act and the Maastricht and Amsterdam Treaties. It is not as fundamentally important as Maastricht; its main focus is on clarification and easing the path to enlargement and further integration that started with Maastricht.

A FEDERAL EUROPE?

You need to know what is meant by a **federal** system of government. The USA, India, Australia and Canada have federal systems. This is where there are two layers of government, each with its own powers and responsibilities.

In the USA, the federal government in Washington, DC, deals with areas such as foreign policy, defence and the national economy, while the separately elected state governments deal with local matters such as education and policing. Each of the two layers is quite separate, yet they work together for the benefit of the people of the USA. There is an independent Supreme Court, which referees disputes between the two layers.

A federal Europe would hand over the 'higher-tier' issues such as international trade and the European economy to Brussels, and leave issues such as education and health care to the national/regional governments.

There is considerable opposition within the EU to any further progress towards a 'federal' Europe.

C Key institutions of the European Union

EUROPEAN COUNCIL

This is the most important decision-maker within the EU. It is made up of the prime ministers and foreign secretaries of all the member states. They meet twice a year. They make the major decisions in areas such as the single European currency and they are responsible for the overall direction of the EU. Countries take it in turns to chair and host the European Council and largely control the agenda.

The central decision-making body of the EU is made up of democratically elected prime ministers, who are responsible to their own electorates.

Note that the UK, like all other countries, is represented on the European Council by two elected representatives — the prime minister and foreign secretary — both of whom can be called to account by their electorate and parliament.

Fundamental changes have to be agreed unanimously by all, but other changes can be passed by a majority vote. The voting is organised so that prime ministers who only represent a small minority of the people in the EU cannot block changes wished by the leaders of the larger and more populous countries.

Major changes like the Maastricht Treaty also have to be accepted by the UK Parliament, and by referendums in some European countries.

The second most
important level of
decision-makers is the
elected ministers of
individual states, such as
the chancellor of the
exchequer.

COUNCIL OF MINISTERS

This is the second most important part of the EU's decision-making process. There are in fact several different Councils of Ministers, each covering a different area of the EU's work, such as agriculture or trade. The membership is made up entirely of the relevant elected ministers from each member state.

For example, the British chancellor of the exchequer will represent the UK when matters of finance are discussed. As with the European Council, the chancellor is elected and can be called to account by the British Parliament and made to defend his or her decisions and votes there.

Once the ministers in the council make a decision, it is handed over to the relevant commissioner to carry out. The executive bodies of the member states are also expected to carry out these decisions.

The voting process
within the EU is
designed both to be
democratic and to
enable action to be
taken.

VOTING IN THE EUROPEAN COUNCIL AND THE COUNCIL OF MINISTERS

Major decisions require agreement by all members, so any nation can stop major changes. Other, more minor matters require a simple majority. Increasingly, however, measures require not unanimity, but a **qualified majority**. This is a system where each member state is given a number of votes roughly in proportion to its population — the UK has ten votes, as do Germany and France, while Denmark has three votes. This stops a single state, which might for example have no major interest in agriculture, preventing something important happening to agriculture in Europe. It takes at least three states — and two of them must be large ones with between eight and ten votes — to block a change.

EUROPEAN COMMISSION

The commission is the civil service of the European Union. A president and 20 commissioners head it. They are not dissimilar in many ways to the cabinet secretary and the permanent undersecretaries who head each government department in the UK, such as the Foreign Office and the Department of Defence. Each commissioner heads a department, such as trade or agriculture, and has a team of assistants.

The commissioners are appointed by the member states. The UK has the right at present to appoint two. They are currently Neil Kinnock, the former Labour leader, who is vice president and in charge of reforming the institutions of the EU, and Chris Patten, a former Conservative minister, who is the 'foreign secretary' of the EU. Their teams are made up of civil servants coming from the member states.

The relationship
between the
commission and the
Council of Ministers
must be known, as
must the role of the
commission.

It is seen as a mark of real quality if a British civil servant is seconded to Brussels for a couple of years. A commissioner and his or her team are expected to serve the EU — not the interests of their own countries — and they are paid out of the EU budget. Their job is to recommend policy and legislation for the Council of Ministers to agree to — or not — and to carry out the instructions of the Council of Ministers. They are expected to have greater influence over the drafting of policy than a British civil servant has: they are really expected to be the driving force of the EU.

Make sure you know the differences between the European Court of Justice and the European Court of Human Rights (see page 123).

EUROPEAN COURT OF JUSTICE

There are at present 15 judges in this court, one from each member state, so there is a British judge there. The European Court of Justice is intended to:

● interpret European law
● solve disputes between members
● sort out complications when European law might come into conflict with the laws of a member state
● impose penalties on member states that choose not to impose European law

In other words, the European Court of Justice is the final arbiter and referee of the EU system and its laws.

EUROPEAN PARLIAMENT

Every member state may elect Members of the European Parliament (MEPs). Numbers vary according to population — the UK currently has the right to elect 87. The European Parliament meets in Strasbourg. Originally it had no power over legislation, but it now has the ability to amend and vet laws made by the Council of Ministers. It has the following powers:

● It may debate all major European legislation.
● It may amend most European legislation.
● It may require the European Council to have unanimity on legislation (not a qualified majority).
● It can veto the EU Budget.
● It can check the work of the European Commission — and has recently insisted on some of the commissioners resigning.

The powers of the European Parliament have grown, but there is a great deal of reluctance on the part of the national parliaments of the member states to give it any more power.

So it has the usual powers of a legislative body, checking the executive, as well as some legislative and financial control. Its ability in these areas has grown considerably since the Single European Act. The Nice Treaty has further enhanced its role in legislation and it is taking its executive scrutiny role much more seriously.

D The impact of the European Union on the United Kingdom

The main effect of the EU is that certain decisions affecting British citizens are now made by British ministers working with other EU ministers in Brussels. The decisions of these European ministers are handed over to the European Commission to carry out (two of the commissioners are chosen by the UK), and their work is monitored by the European Parliament (of which the UK elects 87 members).

Decision making in certain areas, such as agricultural subsidies or aid for failing industries, has been transferred from London (where ministers, civil servants and parliament would in the past have made a decision) to a European decision-making body in Brussels.

Sovereignty in certain specified and agreed areas no longer lies with the British Parliament, but in some areas has been transferred to the European Union. In addition, British courts have to give supremacy to European law and adhere to the European Convention on Human Rights.

The UK has been affected by EU membership in three main areas:

- **Parliament.** The formerly sovereign British Parliament cannot legislate in some areas where sovereignty has been passed to the EU.
- **Executive.** Ministers and civil servants are bound by rules laid down by the European Council and the European Commission, and may have to enforce and obey rulings of the European Court of Justice and the European Court of Human Rights.
- **Judiciary.** Judges have to accept the European Convention on Human Rights as 'superior' to English law. Newspaper publishers in London now have to think much more carefully before publishing material about individuals because of the 'privacy' clauses in the European Convention on Human Rights.

E Attitudes of the major political parties

At the time of writing (August 2001) all three parties are broadly adhering to the policies on the EU laid down in their election manifestos of May 2001. These policies are listed below, but there is a strong possibility that those of both Labour and the Conservatives could change, so careful monitoring of the websites of both parties is recommended.

THE LABOUR PARTY

A significant minority of Labour MPs opposed entry into the EEC in 1972, particularly those on the left of the party. However, Labour prime minister Harold Wilson (1964–70 and 1974–76) was a strong supporter, as was his successor, James Callaghan (1976–79). The Labour Party then moved sharply to the left: the 1983 election manifesto was very hostile to the EEC and committed the party to withdrawal from it if elected. Neil Kinnock, the Labour leader between 1983 and 1992, persuaded the party to change its mind on Europe, and under Tony Blair it has become much more positively pro-EU than the Conservatives are.

When the Labour government was elected in 1997, having promised in its manifesto to be a 'leader in Europe' but to 'oppose a European federal Superstate', it gave the strong appearance of having a much more positive attitude to the EU than John Major's government of 1992–97. Tony Blair signed the Social Chapter, with its minimum wage, and appointed a specific 'minister for Europe'. However, Tony Blair has strongly opposed the federalist agenda wished for by some other Europeans and has also opposed major institutional reforms in the EU designed to give more power to the European Council and the European Commission and to develop a more Europe-wide defence policy. Blair also declined to join the single currency in 1999 when the other members of the EU finally decided to proceed with it.

The Labour Party manifesto of 2001 was prepared to 'engage fully in Europe, help enlarge the EU and make it more effective, and insist that the British people have the final say on any proposal to join the euro'. There was a promise to have a referendum on the single currency early in the next parliament if the five economic preconditions laid down by chancellor of the exchequer Gordon Brown are met. It is felt that the removal of Robin Cook from the post of foreign secretary and his replacement by Jack Straw was a sign of a more cautious attitude towards the EU and the single currency on the part of Tony Blair.

THE CONSERVATIVE PARTY

The main focus of William Hague's 2001 campaign was to 'Keep the Pound'. The Treaty of Nice would be 'renegotiated'. A Conservative government would not participate in any European rapid reaction force that was not under NATO control, and insist on reforming the EU overseas aid programme. Conservative hostility to the euro and to the EU as a whole was an important part of the Hague campaign. The electorate, however, did not see Europe as a major issue.

F Key terms and concepts

Democratic deficit A phrase frequently used by critics of the EU. It is argued that democracy in the UK suffers because unaccountable bureaucrats in Brussels take decisions that affect British citizens, and not elected MPs in the UK, or British civil servants who can be called to account easily. Critics of this view would argue that the main decisions are made by elected ministers and monitored by elected MEPs.

Devolution The granting of power or powers by the 'upper' level of government to a 'lower' one. Of course, what has been granted can be taken back. The British Parliament in Westminster devolved power to the Scottish Parliament in certain specified areas, such as education, but sovereignty remains with the British Parliament — this is the key difference between a system of devolved powers and a federal system.

EMS, EMU and the euro These are complex and very divisive issues, both in politics and in economics.

The European Monetary System (EMS) was devised in the 1980s to stabilise all currencies within the EU and to achieve stable rates of exchange between the currencies of the EU and other major trading partners, such as the USA and Japan. The UK initially joined, but had to withdraw after the recession and currency collapse of 1992 (Black Wednesday) which did so much harm to the government of John Major and damaged plans for further economic integration in the eyes of many.

European monetary union (EMU) and the euro are two of the most complex and divisive issues in British politics at present. Most other countries in the EU have adopted monetary union and the new single European currency, the euro. The UK has declined to join. Monetary union means that there will be a single interest rate covering all EU countries, and that key decisions on issues such as interest rates, inflation and money supply will be taken by a Central European Bank in Frankfurt. For a country to remain in the EMU, its

All candidates are advised to follow the debate on EMU and the euro very carefully, as it is having, and will have, a major impact on almost every other area of the AS Government and Politics specifications.

government must adhere to centrally agreed rules about how much it can borrow. Critics of the EU and defenders of 'national sovereignty' argue strongly against this loss of critical decision making by a national government. The pound would go (as the franc and lira are disappearing) and there would be one single currency throughout Europe.

Enlargement This is the process of adding new member states to the EU. The EU started with six members and has continuously enlarged to include the UK, Ireland and Denmark in 1973 and further countries such as Sweden, Austria and Finland in 1994. The EU — presently comprising 15 members — faces its biggest enlargement decisions in the next few years, with a further 15 states, mainly in eastern Europe and the Baltic, wishing to join. This enlargement would affect the whole structure and operation of the EU.

Federalism A federal system of government is one where there are usually two levels of government, each having sovereignty over certain specified areas. The 'higher' level might take decisions on foreign policy and international trade, as in the case of the USA. The 'lower' level, such as individual states in the USA like California, will take decisions on areas such as education or divorce laws. Again critics of the EU argue that the union is leading towards a 'federal' Europe, where all the key decisions will be made in Brussels, and those decisions will bind all member states. There are plenty of supporters of the EU and its enlargement who are opposed to the idea of a federal Europe; they see a fundamental difference between being a supporter of the EU and a European federalist.

National sovereignty This means that ultimate power lies within the nation. Again, this is a phrase used by critics of the EU who argue that the ability of nations to take their own major decisions has disappeared through membership of the EU, and that the UK has lost its 'national sovereignty'.

Parliamentary sovereignty This means that parliament can do anything except bind its successor. Parliament has the ability to make decisions in any area and it cannot be overruled. It could take the right to vote away from people or reintroduce capital punishment if it wished. However, in both of the cases mentioned it would breach the European Convention on Human Rights, so the UK would have to leave the EU if it wished to enforce them. Parliamentary sovereignty in areas like these has been ceded to the EU.

Sovereignty This is ultimate and final political authority, which cannot be overruled by anyone or any other body. It was always argued that sovereignty in the UK lay with parliament: once it made a law, it bound all to it — even the monarch. As a result of membership of the EU, some of the UK's 'sovereignty' has been transferred to the EU, in certain specified areas. Parliament cannot overrule lawful decisions made by the EU unless the UK withdraws from the EU. It is this loss of partial sovereignty that most concerns critics of British membership of the EU.

Subsidiarity This idea was strongly emphasised in the Maastricht Treaty, but gets very little mention in media coverage of the EU. Subsidiarity means taking decisions at the lowest possible level in an organisation. The EU hoped to defend itself against its critics and the growing 'federal' and 'superstate' arguments by trying to ensure that decisions affecting people in their localities were taken within those localities wherever possible, and not by a 'faceless' or 'unaccountable' bureaucracy in Brussels.

Superstate A term frequently used to characterise the EU by its critics, who see it as dominating the individual states that make up the EU, and overriding the individual interests and individuality of those states, such as the UK. A superstate is seen as an undemocratic and anti-nation force.

For this topic, a detailed knowledge of the structure of the legal system is not required. Edexcel and OCR are both clear in their specifications that they expect knowledge of the judicial system in two areas: first, the impact of the courts and judges on civil liberties (see Unit 14, pages 123–24), and secondly, the relationship between the judicial system (the judges and their courts) and parliament and the executive. This is covered below.

Key questions

What is the role of the judiciary in the British political process?

What is the relationship between the executive and the judicial system in the UK?

Do judges deliver justice and defend freedom?

What is the impact of the courts on the issues of civil liberties and individual rights?

A The role of the judiciary in the United Kingdom

The main role of the judges in the UK is to interpret and administer the law laid down by parliament (statute law) or custom (common law). An example of interpreting the law is that when the law says a police officer may use 'reasonable' force to detain a violent suspect, it is up to a judge to define what is, or is not, reasonable force. An example of administering the law is that when a jury found Jeffrey Archer guilty of perjury, it was the judge's duty to decide on the type and length of sentence.

In theory this is quite a separate function from that of the legislature (parliament) and that of the executive (the prime minister, ministers and the civil service). There is a theoretical **separation of powers** in the UK, so that all three branches of government — executive, legislature and judiciary — can check and balance each other, and thus defend the liberty of the individual in the UK.

In practice, the British judiciary has a vital 'political' role as well as a vital role in defending the rights and liberties of citizens, so how they are appointed and regulated is important.

In practice, however, judges and other parts of the British judicial process, such as the director of public prosecutions who decides who will be prosecuted and for what, have quite 'political' roles. 'Political' in this sense means that the judiciary has to make decisions that affect politicians and political life.

For example, on the day of writing, a judge in the High Court in London was being asked by the mayor of London, Ken Livingstone, whether it was legal for a secretary of state, Steven Byers, to dismiss Bob Kiley from his post as Head of London Transport. Underlying this issue was an even more 'political' debate about whether London Transport was to be owned by the public, or whether it might be partly privatised. Deciding whether a senior member of the Conservative Party who has been in the cabinet, such as Jonathan Aitken, was to be prosecuted, or whether an editor could or could not publish an article or broadcast a programme can also be seen as very 'political' decisions.

THE JUDICIARY AND PARLIAMENT

The ideal situation in a democracy is that judges and parliament should be quite separate, so that each can check the other and therefore protect liberty in the country. If a judge is corrupt, then parliament can dismiss him or her. If parliament makes a law that violates a right laid down in the European Convention on Human Rights, then a judge can declare that law invalid.

Parliament makes laws and judges carry them out. If parliament passes a law saying that all those who commit three major crimes should get a sentence of life imprisonment, then it is the job of the judge to impose that sentence if a jury finds the accused guilty. Parliament votes the funds to pay for the judges, and has the power (never used) to dismiss a judge.

However, in practice the judiciary and parliament are not separate bodies as they are in the USA, where you cannot be both a judge and a member of Congress. The most senior judge in the UK is the lord chancellor, and he or she chairs the House of Lords. The other top judges (the Law Lords) also sit in the House of Lords. In addition, the lord chancellor sits in the cabinet and is therefore a member of the executive.

There is a considerable gap between what should happen in theory in a democracy and what actually happens in practice in the UK.

In theory, parliament has a scrutiny role over the judiciary, but in practice this does not really exist. The lord chancellor, in the House of Lords, usually refuses to answer questions about legal matters. Much the same happens in the House of Commons, where the attorney general, a middle-ranking member of the government, usually declines to answer questions on legal matters. It is worth noting that parliament, which has a large number of lawyers among its membership, is very reluctant to consider a greater scrutiny of the judiciary in the UK. With the present prime minister (and his wife) being lawyers, and with the close relationship between the prime minister and Lord Irvine, the present lord chancellor, there is little likelihood of any major change.

THE JUDICIARY AND THE EXECUTIVE

Again in theory, in order to preserve liberty there should be no formal link between the executive (the government) and the judiciary, as one of the purposes of judges is to preserve the liberties of the citizen against 'bad' government.

In other words, if a police officer (a member of the executive) illegally taps a citizen's telephone, then to gain redress of that grievance, the citizen can take the officer to court. If the police officer's 'boss' — in this case, the home secretary — can in any way harm the judge trying the case, by dismissing the judge, cutting his or her pay, or reducing the judge's promotion prospects, then the judge will not be able to 'judge' fairly.

Again, note the difference between what should happen in theory in a democracy, and the links between the executive and the judiciary in the UK.

One of the strongest criticisms of the judiciary in the UK is that the appointment and promotion of all magistrates and judges lies in the hands of an unelected and unaccountable lord chancellor, who is a key member of the executive and legislature. The fact that the lord chancellor may well sit on many key cabinet committees dealing with 'political' issues, such as the reform of the House of Lords and devolution to Scotland and Wales, gives further grounds for criticism.

THE ROLE OF THE LORD CHANCELLOR

The lord chancellor (who is actually paid more than the prime minister) appoints all judges and magistrates. Senior judges are secretly selected by the lord chancellor, but junior posts are now advertised publicly. The lord chancellor is chair of the House of Lords, and therefore has a key legislative role, and is also a member of the cabinet, and therefore part of the executive.

It is very unusual in a democracy to have one individual who is a member of all three branches of the state — the executive, legislature and judiciary. Constitutional theory states that for there to be genuine liberty for all citizens, the three branches of the state should be quite separate, so that each can prevent the others from acting harshly or illegally.

JUDICIAL REVIEW

This is the ability of judges to **review** (examine) the actions of any public agent, such as a minister, civil servant, police officer or headteacher, and see whether they have acted legally. So if a citizen feels that her telephone has been illegally tapped, or a pressure group feels that a minister has not planned properly for a new motorway, the issue can be taken before a judge, who can prevent the public agent from acting illegally or in an unreasonable way.

Judicial review can also be used to make local government provide a particular type of education for a student. This is a key role for judges — not only to defend the liberties of the citizen, but also to ensure that public agents act within the law.

B Judges and the political process

In theory there should be no 'political' role for judges, but in practice there is. Ministers and their departments can break the law, MPs can be charged with breaking laws about election expenses and civil servants can be charged with handing over secrets about their political 'bosses'. A member of the judiciary has to decide whether they will be charged and, if so, what they will be charged with, and also has to preside over the trial and deal with sentencing if they are found guilty.

Judges' decisions can make life easy or difficult for ministers, MPs and civil servants, so in this respect their decisions are bound to be 'political'. One example was when the Thatcher government tried to ban key civil servants working at GCHQ, the top-secret government communications centre, from joining a trade union. It was a judge who had to rule whether the government had the power to take away this 'right'.

JUDICIAL INDEPENDENCE AND NEUTRALITY

This is an important theory — that all judges must be independent from any outside pressures, such as from a political party or cabinet minister. They may

The lord chancellor is a member of all three branches of government, and therefore breaks the constitutional 'rule' of the separation of powers.

Judicial review is a vital part of the work of judges. Learn one or two recent examples.

Critics of the system argue that judges have now become too 'political' in the UK, and therefore should be made more accountable. Learn some recent examples of their political involvement.

well have to sit in judgement on a politician or a minister, so it is important to the political system that judges are not dependent on politicians or ministers for pay, promotion or keeping their job. Judges' decisions should be made without any fear of reprisal, however unpopular these decisions might be with a government or a political party.

The reasons why the British judiciary is not always seen as independent or neutral should be known.

There are concerns that the most senior judge — the lord chancellor — is essentially a party politician and a member of the executive as well as the legislature (in this case, the House of Lords). Inevitably, there is a fear that appointments and promotions will advance those who favour the lord chancellor's government and party. In addition, there is a concern that the vast majority of judges are:

- male
- white
- elderly
- public school educated
- graduates of Oxford or Cambridge University
- from a wealthy, upper-middle-class background
- products of a legal system where promotion favours the rich and well connected

The feeling of some critics is that the factors listed above mean that judges cannot be independent or neutral, as their thinking is bound to favour other members of the 'establishment' or 'governing classes'.

The method of appointment of judges is also criticised, as there is no open advertisement for senior judges — the lord chancellor takes 'soundings' from other judges about 'suitable' candidates. The lord chancellor's ruling that he will not answer questions on judicial appointments has led to calls for an elected and accountable 'minister of justice', who is not a lawyer, to take charge of the judicial process in the UK, as is the case in other EU countries.

Note also that judges or senior lawyers are frequently used to chair major public inquiries. This important role of the judiciary can again be seen as very 'political'. Examples of these should be known, such as the Lawrence Inquiry into the death of Stephen Lawrence, the Paddington Rail Inquiry and the Kennedy Inquiry into the deaths of babies in Bristol hospitals.

C Key terms and concepts

Judicial independence The independence, or absence of control, of judges from either the legislature (parliament) or the executive, so that neither has a direct influence over the way in which a judge might decide a case or a sentence.

Judicial neutrality The theory that a judge is totally neutral, and therefore because of the absence of any pressure from, for example, ministers, MPs or the media, can make up her or his mind on an issue with complete impartiality. The issue can be judged solely on the merits of the evidence brought before the judge, and will not be influenced by whether the judge might be sacked for giving the 'wrong' decision.

Judicial review The ability of a judge to examine the actions of a member of the executive, or anyone in a position of authority, and rule whether or not the actions were lawful. It can now apply to laws passed by the Westminster Parliament or the Scottish Parliament.

Justice A principle of fairness and proper balance. There is a real difference between what is law and what is 'just'. Justice is done when there has been a proper trial, with a proper defence as well as prosecution, in front of an impartial judge, with a properly chosen jury.

This topic is seen as an important one for both Edexcel and OCR. AQA does not list the British constitution in its specifications, but it is assumed that most of the key points below will be known. You are likely to get direct questions on the topic for both Edexcel and OCR.

Key questions

What is the essential nature of the British constitution?

What are the main sources of the constitution?

What are the merits and demerits of the UK's unwritten constitution?

What important changes have recently taken place to the British constitution?

A Origins and development of the British constitution

DEFINITION

A **constitution** is primarily a set of rules specifying how a country should be governed. Constitutions such as those in France and the USA clearly lay down in writing the powers that the president has, how he or she can be removed, and the president's relationship with the legislative body (parliament) in that country. Matters such as those listed below are usually contained in a constitution:

- elections — how they are conducted
- the relationship between the executive, legislative and judicial parts of government. For example, it is usual to set out exactly what powers the prime minister/president has, and how they can be checked or removed
- usually a statement as to where **sovereignty** (final power) lies. In the case of the USA, it lies with the people
- ways in which the constitution can be changed
- often, lists of what rights citizens have. In the case of the USA, the first ten **amendments** (changes) to the constitution are known as the Bill of Rights, which guarantees freedoms such as the right to a proper trial
- the overall type of government. The American constitution specifies that it will be both a democratic and a federal system

THE BRITISH CONSTITUTION UNDER THE TUDORS

How the UK is governed is the result of a gradual evolution over centuries. The constitutional principle that there ought to be consultation between monarch and people goes back at least as far as the fourteenth century. By 1500, Henry VII fully accepted the need for parliament, with which he could decide major issues. His son Henry VIII moved from Roman Catholicism towards Protestantism not by giving orders like a dictator, but by act of parliament, after consultation with parliament. When Henry VIII executed his wives, they all had a trial first — the constitutional principle of the right to a trial was accepted. By 1550 the superiority of the laws passed by parliament over the

---

Make sure you can give a clear definition of a constitution — and have examples of what it normally contains.

There is a very long tradition of consultation between monarch and people. The idea that everyone must obey the law, including the monarch, is another unwritten 'rule' that goes back centuries.

personal wishes of the king or queen was accepted by everyone, including the monarch. The right to a trial (albeit that it might be rigged) was also seen as part of the British 'constitution' by this time. The constitution was developing and everyone accepted its rules.

THE STUART AND HANOVERIAN PERIODS

The acceptance of the constitution as a sort of gentlemen's agreement, something that few talked about but all understood, came to a halt with the Stuart monarchs. The first two Stuart kings, James I and Charles I, who reigned between 1603 and 1649, wished to end the role of parliament and reassert the role and power of the monarch — in other words, to change the constitution. Parliament's disagreement with this wish led to a civil war and the execution of Charles I. However, the resulting republic did not work well. The lesson learned was that monarch and parliament had to share power sensibly if both were to survive. So new constitutional 'rules' were introduced in the late seventeenth century which implied clear power sharing between parliament and the monarch.

By the end of the eighteenth century:

- A prime minister (living in Downing Street) was accepted by all as the most important decision-maker in Britain.
- A cabinet, all the members of which happened to be members of parliament, helped the prime minister and met regularly to co-ordinate the decision-making process.
- The prime minister and cabinet faced an opposition sitting opposite them in the House of Commons, and they had to answer questions and deal with challenges from that opposition.
- An adverse vote against the prime minister and cabinet in the House of Commons (not the Lords) normally led to the resignation of the government.

These were all parts of the 'constitution'. They were not written down, but they were accepted by all. New 'rules' were being added to the constitution all the time.

THE DEVELOPMENT OF THE CONSTITUTION TO THE PRESENT

The 'rules' of the British constitution continued to adapt and evolve. The power of the monarch continued to decline in the nineteenth century, while the right of the prime minister to appoint ministers and decide on the date of an election became established.

In the twentieth century, there was a huge increase in the size and scope of the government, partly in response to the demands of total war. Women got the vote in 1918, by an act of parliament (another example of how statute law changed the constitution). Nearly universal **suffrage** (voting rights) came simply and quickly in 1918, also by an act of parliament. All of these events changed the constitution.

Unusually, in British political history, the Labour government elected in 1997 promised considerable constitutional reform in its manifesto. This resulted partly from the desire to win votes and partly from successful pressure group politics (e.g. the work of Charter 88). The main commitments made in 1997 were:

- to reform the House of Lords, especially to remove the right of hereditary peers to sit and vote

Note carefully the way in which the constitution adapted to meet contemporary needs.

The constitution continued to change rapidly and adapt to new circumstances throughout the twentieth century. The growing use of the referendum by Tony Blair's government is another example of this.

A good question to consider is the extent to which the Labour governments of 1997 onwards have carried out the manifesto promises of 1997 (see page 117).

- to reform the House of Commons and the way it worked
- to hold referendums on the euro, the way in which London was governed, and devolution to Scotland and Wales
- to adopt the European Convention on Human Rights and make it part of British law
- to bring in a Freedom of Information Act, giving British citizens the right of access to information about themselves and also about the operation of government
- to consider reforming the voting system for general elections in the UK

RECENT DEVELOPMENTS IN THE BRITISH CONSTITUTION

- membership of the EU
- ratification of the Maastricht Treaty
- reform of the House of Lords
- devolution of power to Scotland, Northern Ireland and Wales
- the Human Rights Act
- increased use of referendums in the UK
- the new mayor of London
- increased use of unelected quangos
- the decline in the powers of local government
- 'sleaze'/corruption and the growing demand for reform of the House of Commons

All of these are covered in various parts of this book, but it is vital that you know developments affecting them in the 12 months before you take your examination.

B The main sources of the British constitution

If the UK does not have a written constitution like most other countries, then:
- How do its citizens know what the rules are?
- Where have the rules come from that run the UK?
- Can these rules be changed?
- If so, how can they be changed?

It is not difficult to write down what the main rules are. For example, when a party wins a general election, the constitutional 'rule' is that the leader of that party is asked by the monarch to be the prime minister.

As it happens, there is no piece of paper giving the job specification of a prime minister (whose formal title is 'first lord of the treasury'). Everyone accepts the constitutional 'rule' that it is now the prime minister's job to ask some senior colleagues of the same winning party (who must be members of parliament — another unwritten rule) to belong to the cabinet. Where does the prime minister get the authority to do all this?

The main sources, or origins, of our constitutional rules are:
- the traditional powers of the medieval monarchs — known as the royal prerogatives
- conventions

- common law
- statute law
- written works by well-known experts on the 'constitution'
- the rules of international organisations to which the UK now belongs, such as the EU

These are all explained in detail below.

ROYAL PREROGATIVES

These were the powers that medieval monarchs had, before the days of parliament. They included the powers:

- to declare war or make peace
- to command armies and appoint generals to fight with the monarch
- to appoint ministers
- to raise the money to pay soldiers
- to appoint judges and maintain law and order

Most of the key powers of the prime minister were originally the monarch's.

These were the powers that it was felt necessary for a monarch to have to defend his or her people and ensure their well-being. Over the centuries they have passed from monarch to prime minister, a situation perhaps best illustrated in 1936 when the prime minister, Stanley Baldwin, told the king, Edward VIII, that either he did not marry the divorced Mrs Simpson or the king had to abdicate. Tony Blair might have *informed* the queen that he was sending 'her' troops into Kosovo, but he certainly would not have *consulted* her.

Here are some further examples of the traditional royal prerogative being used by the prime minister:

- Margaret Thatcher's decision to send troops to the Falklands
- John Major's negotiation of the Maastricht Treaty
- Tony Blair's decision about the date of the general election in 2001
- Tony Blair's decision to reshuffle his cabinet entirely after winning the general election of 2001. For example, he removed Robin Cook from the role of foreign secretary and made him leader of the House of Commons

CONVENTIONS

The best definition of a convention is that it is an unwritten rule or custom, which is known to all, accepted by all, and followed by all.

'Ministerial responsibility' is a good example of this. There is no law which lays down that a minister is responsible for everything his or her department does, but all ministers accept it. A further part of this convention is that if a minister makes a major error of judgement, then that minister will resign. A good example of this is that when Peter Mandelson, secretary of state for trade and industry, was discovered to have 'forgotten' to declare the loan of a large sum of money from another minister to buy a house, he resigned.

A huge part of the British constitution is not written in any form, but is just accepted practice.

Other examples of important constitutional conventions are:

- Collective responsibility is taken, where the whole cabinet accepts responsibility for, and supports in public, a decision made by any member of the cabinet.
- The monarch accepts the advice of the prime minister.
- The monarch always signs bills that are agreed by both Houses of Parliament.

- It has now become a convention that major changes to the constitution, such as devolution, will be put to a referendum before parliament acts on them.

COMMON LAW

This is law based on the rulings made by judges when dealing with cases where there is no clear statute law (see below). It was a judge who ruled that suspects had a right of silence in criminal cases. It was another judge who ruled in the 1770s that slavery could not exist in Britain.

Many of these rulings by judges gave British citizens the rights that are normally laid down in written constitutions. Their decisions became part of the rules that affect the way in which the UK is governed.

STATUTE LAW

This is law passed by both Houses of Parliament and signed by the monarch. As early as 1500 everyone accepted that this was the supreme form of law and could overrule, for example, the wishes of the monarch or a custom that had been around for centuries. The courts, the police and the government must enforce this type of law, which is known as an act of parliament when agreed by all three parts of parliament: the Commons, the Lords and the monarch. A large number of acts play a very important part in making up the constitution. Examples are:

- the Mutiny Act, which gives military officers the right to give orders to and discipline soldiers
- the Parliament Act, which rules that there has to be a general election at least every five years
- the Human Rights Act, which guarantees many basic freedoms

Everyone must obey all of these acts, many of which are normally written into the constitutions of other countries.

WRITTEN WORKS BY CONSTITUTIONAL EXPERTS

These are books by accepted experts on the constitution, or parts of it. Very often they simply contain what everyone knows is supposed to happen, but they do it in a clear form so that newcomers to politics and government can actually read 'the constitution'.

A good example of this is Bagehot's *The British Constitution*, written in the last part of the nineteenth century. He describes clearly what the role of the cabinet, parliament and the monarch then was. What he did was put on paper what everyone knew was right in practice. Other important texts are Erskine May's *Parliamentary Practice*, which explains how parliament works, and Dicey's *Study of the Law of the Constitution*, which analyses in depth such areas as the exact relationship between judges and the government.

MEMBERSHIP OF INTERNATIONAL ORGANISATIONS SUCH AS THE EUROPEAN UNION

Membership of the EU has also altered the British constitution. When we joined it, we accepted that some of the rules by which we are governed would now be made in Brussels. We agreed to give up our sovereignty in specified areas in order to gain the benefits of membership of this 'club'.

Common law is another example of the constantly changing and unwritten aspects of the British constitution.

Statute law gives a government with a majority in parliament the ability to change the constitution of the UK very easily, as devolution to Scotland shows.

Written works by constitutional experts play an important role in explaining and clarifying current constitutional practice.

In the past, we accepted that the British Parliament was sovereign in all matters. Then, by passing a statute law, parliament changed the British constitution to give the EU some powers to make rules that bind all British citizens. The EU now decides the size of lorries allowed on our roads, for example. Other European countries, such as Ireland, can only change their constitution by a referendum in which all the people of that country are consulted, while in the UK the constitution can be changed just by passing an act of parliament.

Membership of the EU has led to huge constitutional changes.

C Principles of the British constitution

The American constitution states that the reason for the constitution's existence is to enable the American people to have 'life, liberty and the pursuit of happiness'. With no written constitution in the UK, there is a debate about what the underlying principles and purpose of the unwritten British constitution are. In theory, however, they are supposed to be:

- the sovereignty of parliament
- the rule of law
- the unitary state
- the separation of powers
- responsible government

The ability to explain clearly these underlying constitutional principles is very important.

THE SOVEREIGNTY OF PARLIAMENT

Quite simply this means that the British Parliament is the UK's sovereign body. This means that it has absolute power over everyone in the country. It can pass a law that enables the UK to join the EU, but it can also pass a law that takes it out again. It can bring back capital punishment and allow the state to execute citizens, or it can take away the right of a woman to have an abortion. Now that specific powers have been given to the Scottish Parliament and to the European Commission, parliament has reduced its sovereignty, but it can regain it if it wishes.

The sovereignty of parliament remains one of the most important principles of the British constitution, and with the possibility of much more power going to the EU, it is being strongly debated at present.

The use of referendums to consult people, instead of parliament just taking the decisions, may also have reduced parliament's sovereignty. However, there is nothing present in the British constitution to make parliament call any more referendums.

THE RULE OF LAW

Quite simply this means that 'law rules'. It also means that in the UK all citizens are under the law, and that includes the monarch and members of the government. All must obey the law and all should be equal before it. Government, the police and everyone acting in an official capacity must obey the law and recognise the legal rights of the people they are supposed to be serving. This means that all accused citizens are entitled to their day in court, and to have a fair trial. It also means that a citizen can take members of the government to court if they believe they have acted against the law, or exceeded the powers that parliament

This principle is vital in regulating the conduct of government and in ensuring democracy and human rights.

gave them. It also states that judges ought to be independent from political control, and obey the law and not the government. As seen in Unit 12, this does not quite happen in the UK.

A case where the original theory is becoming very much altered in practice.

THE UNITARY STATE

A unitary state is a state where one body holds all the important powers. In the case of the UK, this is parliament and the government in London. Whatever powers might be given to other bodies, say to the mayor of London or the Scottish Parliament, are given by parliament and can be taken away again. However, note the changes resulting from the devolved powers to the Scottish Parliament and to the European Union. The principle of the unitary state is evidently decreasing in importance.

THE SEPARATION OF POWERS

This is an old idea that is fine in theory, but which never seems to have actually worked in practice in the UK. The idea was originally that the three 'powers' — the executive, the legislature and the judiciary — should always be quite separate. No one person should be a member of more than one of these parts of government. The idea was that for citizens to have freedom and protection from a bad government, an incompetent parliament or a biased judge, each of the three parts should have a checking role on the others. Parliament, for example, could get rid of a bad judge or an incompetent minister; a judge could imprison a corrupt minister.

The substantial gap between theory and practice in the separation of powers must be clearly understood.

However, practice is now divorced from theory in that, by convention, British ministers all sit in parliament, and the top judge — the lord chancellor — sits in the House of Lords and is also a member of the government. No one is quite sure why the practice has become so far removed from the theory!

RESPONSIBLE GOVERNMENT

This principle is derived from two conventions mentioned earlier: ministerial responsibility and collective cabinet responsibility. It means that the government must take responsibility for its actions. The right of citizens to call a minister to account for his or her actions is a vital part of British democracy. This is also known as the principle of **accountability**.

D The constitution: a major issue

The reasons for major constitutional change are a very likely question.

The constitution has become an important issue in recent years. Since about 1970 many different groups have suggested that the constitution should be both changed and written down clearly. There are many reasons for this. The main ones are:

- a growing dislike of British methods of election, which many saw as 'unfair'
- the fact that no party since the war has had a majority of the electorate vote for it

- growing demands by Scottish, Welsh and Northern Irish people for less control from London
- a growing dislike of the role and influence of the unelected monarchy and the unelected House of Lords
- the changes that membership of the EU was bringing to the British system of government
- a growing concern that individual liberty was being reduced and that the government was growing too powerful
- a genuine wish to have a clear, simple and written constitution that all knew and understood

RECENT CONSTITUTIONAL CHANGES

The Labour government elected in 1997 had promised in its manifesto to make constitutional changes. It has delivered on some of its promises, but its critics argue that it has not gone as far as it should have. The changes it has made (by statute) are as follows:

- It has reformed the House of Lords. The right of the hereditary peers to sit and vote in the House of Lords has been abolished.
- It has devolved power to Scotland, Wales and Northern Ireland. Scotland has its own parliament and Wales and Northern Ireland their own assemblies.
- It has altered the electoral system in Scotland, Wales and Northern Ireland. Proportional representation has been introduced.
- It has held binding referendums in Scotland, Wales and Northern Ireland.
- It has brought in the Human Rights Act, which guarantees liberties to citizens.
- It has set up the new lord mayor of London with devolved powers.

This is more than any government has done since before the First World War.

The nature and extent of the constitutional changes brought in by Tony Blair's government since 1997 have to be known in detail.

CRITICISMS OF THE RECENT CONSTITUTIONAL CHANGES

- The Labour government has not reformed the House of Commons in a meaningful way. It had been suggested that the government would give select committees much more power to scrutinise the executive and also make parliament work more sensible hours and not late at night. These changes have not happened. In fact, the government increased its hold and influence over parliament, and it has been argued that it largely ignored parliament because it had such a large majority in the Commons.
- It has not changed the voting system for general elections in the UK. Tony Blair failed to get a majority of the electorate to vote for him in 1997, yet he still had a huge majority in the Commons.
- It has not fully tackled the problem of the House of Lords. It has not reformed the role of the Lords. In addition, peers are still not elected and many of Tony Blair's appointments seem to be strong supporters of the Labour government.
- It has not given citizens the freedom to acquire the information they want about themselves or their government's actions. Labour had promised a Freedom of Information Act, but this has not been forthcoming.
- It has not really sorted out the relationship between the government in London and those in Edinburgh, Cardiff and Belfast.
- There is still no written constitution in the UK.

SHOULD THE UK HAVE A WRITTEN CONSTITUTION?

Arguments for:

- Everyone would know exactly what a government can and cannot do.
- It would stop government from becoming too powerful.
- It would give the UK the opportunity to get rid of out-of-date parts of its constitution, such as a hereditary monarchy.
- Everyone would know their rights.
- It would end the odd system where the underlying theories, such as the separation of powers, do not match up with current practice.

Arguments against:

- The present system actually works well — it is flexible and people like it.
- There is no demand for much change.
- There would be no real agreement on what should replace the existing system.
- We would lose the great flexibility we have. We can change the rules quickly if we want to.
- Other countries have tremendous difficulties in changing their written constitutions when change is needed.

E Key terms and concepts

Authority The right or ability to have proposals or wishes accepted. For example, parliament may give a minister the authority to decide on a motorway route. However, authority can also be a variable, in that a prime minister who has successfully won a second election may have increased authority over his or her party.

Common law Law made by ordinary judges, making a ruling on a case that has come before them. A recent example was a ruling that a local authority had the power compulsorily to sterilise a mentally handicapped young woman in its care.

Constitutional government A government that accepts the limits imposed by a constitution, and either works within the written guidelines laid down by the constitution (as in France and the USA) or accepts the unwritten guidelines (as in the UK). An example of this is Tony Blair only having ministers who are members of parliament, although there is no written rule that says ministers have to be members of the House of Commons or the House of Lords.

Convention A long-established custom or tradition, which is now so accepted that it has the same 'force' as a law. It is now an established convention that the decision to go to war (as when Tony Blair ordered the bombing of Serbia and sent British troops into Kosovo) is taken by the prime minister, even though it is part of the royal prerogative.

Executive The decision-making/administrative part of a political system — the prime minister, the cabinet and the civil service in the UK; the president in France.

Government The lawfully elected group which heads the executive and is responsible to parliament. In the UK this refers to the prime minister, his or her ministers and the civil servants who work for them.

Don't confuse government with parliament, state or party — that can cause real concern in the mind of an examiner about your overall understanding.

Judiciary The part of the system that interprets and administers the law — the lord chancellor, the judges and the magistrates in the UK.

Legislature The body that makes laws in a country — parliament in the UK; Congress in the USA.

Parliamentary sovereignty Where sovereignty (absolute power) lies with parliament. In theory this means that parliament can do anything, and cannot be overruled. It can pass a law making it compulsory for everyone to wear seat belts in cars, for example. However, membership of the EU has restricted parliamentary sovereignty, as decisions in some areas have gone to the EU.

Power The ability to make people do things, some of which they may not want to do. The prime minister of the UK has the power to dismiss a cabinet minister, even though that cabinet minister may wish to stay in office. The prime minister could have that decision backed up by force if need be.

Royal prerogatives The traditional powers and privileges of monarchs, such as to make war and peace, and to act as the head of the executive in the country.

Sovereignty Ultimate power and authority in a system. The sovereign power is the final decision-maker, which cannot be overruled by anyone. Don't confuse this with the 'sovereign' — another name for the monarch. In the American constitution it is made clear that sovereignty lies with 'the people'.

Don't confuse the state with government or the executive — they are both part of the state.

State The complete system through which people are governed and administered — government, parliament, police, local government, the education system, judges and so on.

Statute law Laws that are made by parliament, passed by both the House of Commons and the House of Lords, and signed by the monarch. The act passed in 1972 that led to the United Kingdom joining the European Union is a good example of a statute law that radically changed the constitution.

This is a series of interconnected topics that are listed in the specifications of all three examination boards. There is also a strong possibility that a question will link this topic to the judiciary, so both topics should be revised together (see Unit 12). Edexcel and OCR give these topics a higher priority than AQA, so there is a greater chance of these exam boards asking a specific question on them.

Key questions

What is citizenship? What are the rights and duties of a citizen?

What rights and liberties are, and should be, enjoyed by British citizens?

How well are civil rights and liberties protected in the UK?

How well are grievances of citizens redressed in the UK?

A Citizenship

This definition must be known.

DEFINITION

A citizen is a member of a state. Citizenship defines the legal relationship between the state and an individual. Being a citizen of a state implies both rights and duties. A citizen of the UK has the right to be protected by the police, but also has a duty to support the police and pay taxes.

Be able to differentiate clearly between a citizen's rights and duties.

THE RIGHTS OF A CITIZEN

These will vary from state to state, but in the UK they include such factors as the protection of the law, the right to own property and freedom of movement. Other rights might be seen as healthcare and social security in time of need. Definitions may well vary according to opinion: for example, some will argue that there is a right to work, while others may see work as a duty.

The duties of a citizen have become a major priority of the present government.

THE DUTIES OF CITIZENSHIP

There is a strong move by the current Labour government to emphasise the duties of a citizen. The Conservatives started this process in the 1980s. In this context, a duty means what a citizen gives to the state as part of the price of membership of that state — rather like a subscription to a club that an individual may join. This not only includes obvious duties such as the duty to do jury service or to fight in time of war, but also the duty:

- to vote in all elections — European, national and local
- to help the police deal with crime
- to get work and provide for one's own old age, and not rely totally on a state pension
- to help the local community
- to get involved in major social and political issues
- to be involved in voluntary and charitable work
- generally to take personal responsibility for oneself, one's family and the community at large

This represents a considerable shift in position for the Labour Party. In the past,

'Old Labour' placed much more emphasis on state provision, and much less on individuals providing for themselves. This change is very much part of the 'New Labour' agenda.

THE CITIZEN'S CHARTER

Although it was much criticised at the time, the Citizen's Charter was an important step forward in the rights and responsibilities of citizens.

The government of John Major recognised that government was failing to solve many problems, such as homelessness and rising juvenile crime. It felt that the solution to such concerns might lie with individual citizens involving themselves much more actively in a local community. As a result it introduced the Citizen's Charter, which focused primarily on the rights of citizens. The key features of the Citizen's Charter were as follows:

- Clear performance targets were to be set by public services (e.g. passport offices) in order to improve service to citizens. Citizens had a 'right' to quality public services.
- Known means of gaining redress for their grievances were made available to citizens who did not get quality service. If your train was late, or your holiday was delayed because you had to wait so long for a passport, then you would be compensated.
- There was to be public and formal recognition of those public services, such as transport or healthcare, that attained or bettered their improvement targets.

NEW LABOUR AND CITIZENSHIP

The initial focus on the rights of citizens in the Citizen's Charter of John Major is now being shifted by Tony Blair more on to the duties of citizens.

Tony Blair's government since 1997 has placed a stronger emphasis on citizenship. It has continued to emphasise the rights of citizens (e.g. introducing the minimum wage and incorporating the European Convention on Human Rights in the laws of the UK), but there has also been a greater focus on the duties of citizens. For example:

- The 'Welfare to Work' programme encouraged citizens to get work rather than seek state benefits. This placed much more responsibility on the unemployed to look actively for work, and penalised those who did not. It was quite a radical step for a Labour government.
- Parents were encouraged to take more responsibility for their children, particularly in areas such as juvenile crime and school attendance.
- Compulsory 'education for citizenship' was introduced in schools, with a particular focus on the need for the individual to be involved in the community.

B Rights and liberties

THE DEVELOPMENT OF RIGHTS AND LIBERTIES IN THE UK

There has never been a clear statement of the rights and liberties of British citizens.

It was the custom in England for individuals to have the right to do what they wished unless there was a law against it. Sometimes acts of parliament were passed to take away rights, such as the freedom from arrest without due cause, in time of war. At other times, parliament might pass a law giving citizens new rights, such as the right to vote in secret in 1872. The rights and liberties of British citizens never developed in an organised or systematic way. People were used to having no clear definition of their rights, such as the Americans have in the first ten amendments to their constitution, known as the Bill of Rights.

In the 1980s the issue of citizens' rights and liberties became much more widely publicised, and this has pressured the government into action.

THREATS TO RIGHTS AND LIBERTIES IN THE 1980s

The issue of the lack of clearly defined citizens' rights became more prominent in the 1980s under the government of Margaret Thatcher. In several areas what had been seen as traditional 'rights' appeared to be under threat. These were:

- **The right to silence.** There was uncertainty about how secure the citizen's right to remain silent after arrest was, and whether it actually was a 'right'.
- **Freedom of the press.** There was a strong feeling that the Official Secrets Act stopped the press and other media from doing their 'duty' in checking the government. There was also concern that the rich and powerful, such as the newspaper owner Robert Maxwell and the Conservative politician Jeffrey Archer, could use the threat of libel and slander laws to stop unfavourable (but true) items being published about them.
- **Freedom to broadcast.** The government was able to ban radio or television shows that it felt might damage state security (but might also reveal its own incompetence!). It also prevented broadcasters from having representatives of Sinn Fein, one of the main nationalist parties in Northern Ireland, speaking on television and radio.
- **The right to privacy.** Many 'public' figures, including the royal family, resented the frequent intrusions, comments and photographs about them in the media, sometimes in very unflattering situations. At the same time, legislation was passed that gave the police and the security services much easier access to telephone conversations.
- **Freedom of information.** Citizens did not have access to information held about them, such as medical records — or UCAS references!

THE EUROPEAN CONVENTION ON HUMAN RIGHTS

Many argue that the greatest constitutional change that the Labour government elected in 1997 brought about is the full acceptance of the European Convention on Human Rights and its incorporation into the law of the land. Critics see this acceptance, which was implemented through the Human Rights Act of 1999, as an important loss of national sovereignty, as British judges and parliament are now bound by it.

You must know the basic terms of this convention, which is now part of the laws of the UK. These terms are a vital part of the whole 'rights and liberties' topic.

The main terms of the convention are:
- the right to life
- freedom from torture
- the right to liberty and security of person
- the right to a fair trial by an impartial tribunal
- the right to respect for private and family life, home and correspondence
- freedom of thought and expression
- the right to an effective remedy against authority, such as a government
- freedom from discrimination

There are also some additions, known as protocols. The main ones are:
- the right to education
- the right to take part in free elections with a secret ballot

This convention, together with the UK's obedience to decisions made by the European Court of Human Rights, has had a major impact on the rights and liberties of citizens in the UK. It has ensured that women workers get equal pay for equal work and have the same retirement age as men. It has affected the way in which police may interrogate suspects and the procedures for school children getting expelled or suspended from school.

It is of huge importance and it will take some years before the full implications are realised. Newspaper editors, while delighted about the 'freedom of expression' part of the convention, are much less enthusiastic about the right of privacy, which they feel might limit their ability to investigate politicians such as Jonathan Aitken and Jeffrey Archer in the way that they did, and to expose their failings.

THE EUROPEAN COURT OF HUMAN RIGHTS

If British citizens feel that any of their rights under the European Convention have been violated, then they are fully entitled to take the issue to the European Court of Human Rights if they cannot get redress in the British courts.

This has happened frequently in the past, and in several cases the European Court of Human Rights has ruled that an action of the British government was 'illegal'.

Two examples of this are:
- when the European Court stopped corporal punishment in British schools although the British government had permitted it
- when the European Court ruled that particular methods used by the British government in Northern Ireland to interrogate IRA suspects were 'torture', and had to be stopped

> The European Court of Human Rights has played and is playing a critically important role in ensuring that British citizens' rights are fully protected.

Defence of rights and liberties in the UK

Candidates need to know the main ways in which a citizen who has had one of his or her 'rights', such as freedom of expression, violated can practise that right freely and, if necessary, can claim compensation for that violation.

THE ROLE OF THE JUDICIARY

The principal defenders of citizens' rights are the courts of law. If a citizen feels that a policewoman has exceeded her authority and detained them for too long, or an editor feels that he is being prevented from publishing an article critical of a minister, they can go to court.

It is possible for a judge to declare that the action of the policewoman was wrong, or that the article should be published. If the citizen does not like the ruling of the English judge, he or she can appeal to the European Court of Human Rights — and if that court feels that the English judge was wrong, and the citizen's rights were violated, then it can overturn the English judge's ruling, and English courts have to obey that decision.

The role of the judges is vital here. Two examples are as follows:
- A judge ruled that an operation to separate Siamese twins could go ahead, even though it would certainly lead to the death of one of them. The judge had to

consider the rights and wishes of the parents, who opposed the operation, and the rights of the twin who might live, and the rights of the twin who would die.

- Judges had to decide whether farmers had the 'right' to resist Ministry of Agriculture officials coming on to their land to slaughter animals possibly infected with foot-and-mouth disease.

There is always a concern that the process can be slow and very expensive, and this deters many individuals. Pursuing a case right through to the European Court of Human Rights can take several years and the costs can run well into six or seven figures.

THE ROLE OF PARLIAMENT

Another possible defender of the rights of the citizen is parliament. Constituents have a right to see their MP, either in Westminster or in the MP's 'surgery' in their constituency. MPs do not have extensive powers individually, but they do have some powers to protect people's rights:

- MPs can write directly to a minister or a government department, agency or quango. It is expected that an MP's complaint will be taken seriously and replied to. Many minor issues, such as the non-payment of money owed to citizens by the Inland Revenue, or disability pensions, are dealt with effectively at this level.
- They can question a minister orally at Question Time or put down a written question. The latter tends to be more effective, particularly in miscarriage of justice cases.
- They can raise the matter as an adjournment debate at the end of a parliamentary day. This tends to be most effective when dealing with issues affecting groups of constituents — consider, for example, the way in which MPs from rural constituencies used it to protect farmers in the foot-and-mouth crisis.
- They can refer a matter to the ombudsman or a parliamentary select committee. The ombudsman (the parliamentary commissioner for administration) does have some investigative powers (see Unit 7, page 61).

On the whole, however, the scope for MPs is fairly limited, unless they are part of a wider campaign. The example of Chris Mullin MP and the wrongful conviction of the Birmingham Six shows this.

THE ROLE OF THE MEDIA

Sympathetic and widespread coverage by the media can also help to defend citizens' rights. Two good examples in 2000 were sympathetic media coverage of the campaign to increase old age pensions and of the fuel tax protest, which arguably played an important role in changing government policy.

ADMINISTRATIVE TRIBUNALS

These are independent bodies, set up by government, designed to deal with specific grievances a citizen may have against a government department or an employer. They are free, impartial and relatively quick. They cover areas such as tax, pensions, compensation for property being taken over to build motorways, unfair dismissal at work, denial of equal opportunities, and racial discrimination. Citizens' Advice Bureaux in most towns will help people to access these tribunals — they tend to know more about these things than even MPs.

The courts, both British and European, are vital in the defence of a citizen's rights. Learn several recent examples.

Look at the House of Commons website for recent examples.

Look at the ombudsman's website and learn a couple of examples.

Administrative tribunals are little-known, but vital, methods by which a citizen can gain redress of grievances in many different areas.

If, for example, a citizen feels that she has not been fairly compensated by government for having a motorway put through her land, then she can appeal to the relevant administrative tribunal. It is chaired by an independent lawyer, and will have two specialists in land values/property on it, as well as two local 'lay' people, who are chosen for their common sense and good judgement rather than for any specialist knowledge.

The citizen makes her case before it, assisted by a 'friend' or lawyer if she wishes. The relevant government department's official replies — the reply must be in non-technical language — and then the tribunal makes its decision. It can order compensation to be paid if it considers this appropriate. There is, of course, a right of appeal to the courts if the citizen is unhappy with the decision.

The biggest area of growth for administrative tribunals now lies with those who feel they have been discriminated against at work on grounds of race or sex, or have been unfairly dismissed by an employer.

PUBLIC INQUIRIES

The key problem with public inquiries is that governments do not have to carry out the inquiries' recommendations.

Citizens unhappy with the actions of government or other bodies such as the police or railways can pressurise government directly for a public inquiry. Good examples of this are the Lawrence Inquiry into the way in which the police dealt with the murder of Stephen Lawrence, and the public inquiry into the Paddington rail crash. A more recent example is the inquiry led by a well-known lawyer, Ian Kennedy, into the number of babies who had died after heart surgery in a Bristol hospital. Inquiries may recommend action, but there is no requirement on government to implement their recommendations.

THE ROLE OF THE LOCAL COUNCILLOR

Citizens who have a grievance that comes under the jurisdiction of the local council — in areas such as education, planning and housing — need to see their local councillor in the same way as they should see their MP on national matters. Local councillors have similar influence and there is also access to the local government ombudsman. Because of a lack of public awareness of what a council (or councillor) can and cannot do, limited use is made of them.

THE ROLE OF PRESSURE GROUPS

These are playing an increasing role in enabling individual citizens or groups of citizens to gain redress of grievances or uphold their rights. There are many examples, ranging from those who form a pressure group to stop a motorway crossing their land (e.g. the building of the M40 north of Oxford) to the group of concerned and distressed parents in the Bristol area who felt that their babies had died unnecessarily through bungled heart surgery. The latter managed to get a public inquiry (see above), compensation and the dismissal of the surgeons involved.

D Key terms and concepts

Active citizenship This implies that a citizen will not only benefit fully from the rights and privileges given to citizens, such as the protection of the law, but also take a serious and wide-ranging role in fulfilling the duties of a citizen. This includes voting in all elections, assisting in the upholding of the law and helping to improve the quality of life in a community.

Citizenship The status of being a citizen. The law of a country will lay down the qualifications required for being a citizen. Citizenship implies the willingness to participate in the running of the state as well as benefiting from the privileges given to a citizen of a state.

Civil liberties The freedoms that are, or should be, guaranteed to individuals in a state to protect them against harsh treatment. The right to silence and the right to a fair trial are typical 'civil liberties'.

Duties The actual responsibilities of being a citizen. For example, all citizens should see it as their duty to vote and assist in the upholding of the law.

Liberties The simplest definition of liberties is the kind of actions that are considered acceptable by the society you live in. Law may define them, but it is normally 'rights' that are laid down by law.

Obligations Another much debated term. The simplest definition of an obligation is something that a citizen ought to do, such as pay taxes properly, without any persuasion. Citizens ought to fulfil their obligations to a state, as they are members of that state.

Political participation Literally, taking part in politics. Participation is normally measured by the number of citizens who vote in all elections and join political parties.

Rights Possibly one of the most debated words in politics! A right is the ability to do something, which may well be guaranteed by law. The European Convention on Human Rights gives everyone a right to marry. Some writers argue that your rights, such as the right to life, are so fundamental that they cannot be taken away or altered in any way by laws passed in parliament.